D1286833

IN PARABLES

BOOKS BY THE SAME AUTHOR . . .

LIVING WITH ROYALTY
SERMONS ON SIMON PETER
SERMONS FROM JOB
MEET THESE MEN
THE SEVEN WORDS
ANOINTED TO PREACH
WHEN THE CHURCH WAS YOUNG
QUESTIONS JESUS ASKED
AND THE PROPHETS
IF I WERE YOUNG
LIVING ZESTFULLY
SERMONS FROM REVELATION
FEMININE FACES
FACES ABOUT THE CROSS
THE ROAD TO CERTAINTY
VALUES THAT LAST
TEN RULES FOR LIVING
SERMONS FROM THE MIRACLES
CHAPPELL'S SPECIAL DAY SERMONS
SERMONS ON THE LORD'S PRAYER
SERMONS FROM THE PARABLES
SERMONS FROM THE PSALMS
THE SERMON ON THE MOUNT
THE VILLAGE TRAGEDY
THE CROSS BEFORE CALVARY

IN
PARABLES

CLOVIS G. CHAPPELL

ABINGDON PRESS

New York • *Nashville*

IN PARABLES

Copyright MCMLIII by Pierce & Washabaugh

All rights in this book are reserved.
No part of the book may be reproduced in any
manner whatsoever without written permission of
the publishers except brief quotations embodied in
critical articles or reviews. For information address
Abingdon Press, Nashville 2, Tennessee.

Library of Congress Catalog Number: 53-8132

c

SET UP, PRINTED, AND BOUND BY THE
PARTHENON PRESS, AT NASHVILLE,
TENNESSEE, UNITED STATES OF AMERICA

To

THOMAS HART

my oldest and youngest grandson

CONTENTS

IN PARABLES

I

HOW GOD MEETS OUR NEEDS

"He will rise and give him as many as he needeth."

LUKE 11:8

"HE WILL RISE AND GIVE HIM AS MANY AS HE NEEDETH."
This is the climax to a story that Jesus told his
disciples in answer to their questions about prayer.
Captivated by the beauty and worth of the prayer life
of their Lord, they had come to him with this wise
request, "Lord, teach us to pray." In reply Jesus, instead
of giving them a few rules, a few fixed precepts, spoke
to them in the universal language of humanity. That
is, he told them a story.

This story is a very homely story. It comes right out
of life. It is something that might have happened to
any villager of that day. It has a touch of comedy in it
as the discerning eye can see. It also has a touch of
tragedy and of triumph. There are those who frown
upon anything in the pulpit that smacks of the emotional, but to bypass the emotional altogether is to
bypass life. This is the case because life is largely woven

9

out of the warp and woof of laughter and of tears. Jesus brought this story to a conclusion by saying that in answer to prayer God will meet all our needs.

I

Now notice that this promise has its limits.

Jesus is not telling us that in answer to prayer God will grant our every wish. If we, as children, had received the gratification of our every wish, the chances are that we would never have become of age. There is too wide a chasm between what we wish and what we really need. As a boy I once found myself a half day's journey from home at lunch time without any lunch. But, being a thrifty lad, I had a five-cent piece. I considered carefully what I would buy for my lunch and decided that what I wished above all else was a smoke. I had never smoked in my life. Well, I smoked the cigar that I bought with that money on what I thought was an empty stomach. I found that I was slightly mistaken. I also found that while I eagerly wished for a cigar that cigar did not meet my needs.

If prayer were a way of so tugging at God's skirts that he would give up his will for our will, if prayer were a way of getting gratification for our every wish and for our every whim, then it would be the most deadly dangerous thing in the world. Not only would it wreck us, but it would wreck those about us. Jesus does not promise that God will grant every wish in answer to our prayers, however earnest those prayers may be.

No more does he promise that in answer to prayer God will grant everything that we honestly think we need. Sometimes we are vastly mistaken about what our needs are. Even as great a saint as Paul was so mistaken. He had a thorn in the flesh. Whatever that thorn was, it embarrassed him. He felt that he could carry on his work in the world so much better without it. Therefore he hurried with all boldness into the presence of his Lord asking for its removal. God answered his prayer, but he did not grant his request. I can imagine that at first Paul was keenly disappointed, but his disappointment did not last. He discovered in later days that what had seemed to be a source of want had become a source of unspeakable wealth. Therefore he came to thank God earnestly for leaving him with his thorn.

It would seem that at one time even Jesus was uncertain as to what the will of God was for his own life. It was hard for him to believe that the cross was the Father's will for him. Therefore he said: "Now is my soul troubled; and what shall I say? Father, save me from this hour: But for this cause came I unto this hour. Father, glorify thy name." That was just another way of saying, "Since this cup may not pass from me except I drink it, thy will be done." God does not promise to give us everything that we think we need because we are sometimes so vastly mistaken as to what our needs are.

What God does promise is this, to use the words of Paul, "My God shall supply all your needs according to his riches in glory in Christ Jesus." That sounds like

11

a big order. It sounds extravagant. In fact it is the very best that God can offer. It even sounds too good to be true when we look at ourselves with our multitudinous needs. But when we look at God, when we realize that he is able to do exceeding abundantly above all that we ask or think, it no longer seems to be too good to be true. On the contrary, it seems too good not to be true. So here is his promise and he stands back of every syllable of it, "He will rise and give him as many as he needeth."

II

By this simple story Jesus tells us how we are to pray in order to give God the opportunity to meet our needs.

The first step in prayer is a sense of need. We may pour out whole rivers of words without any sense of need, but before we really pray there must be a need. That was the case with this host. He had a guest who had come at midnight. He was unexpected and therefore there was no provision made for his entertainment. Since it was midnight, there was no market where this man with his empty cupboard might buy bread. Therefore he was up against it. It seemed that there was nothing he could do about it. But he was a resolute man. Besides he cared deeply for his guest. Therefore he did not shrug his shoulders and say, "There is nothing I can do about it." He did not give way to that very imperfect virtue that we call resignation.

Instead he stood scanning the horizon of his possibilities as a shipwrecked sailor might scan the sea in

the hope of seeing a friendly sail. By and by, I see
the gloom of his face give way to gladness. I think he
must have laughed softly to himself. "Why didn't I
think of him before?" he says in an undertone. "My
old friend, Simon, he has plenty of bread. I never
knew him to be short. Besides, being my friend, he will
be willing to give me bread. He will be willing in spite
of the lateness of the hour. I am not in this thing alone.
I have a friend who will share it with me. Therefore, in
spite of my embarrassment, I can yet come out with
flying colors."

How did this embarrassed host come to think of his
friend just at this time? It may be that he had spoken
to him not two days before. It may be that he had not
spoken to him for a week or a month. But how did
he come to remember him? He remembered him because he was in need. He remembered him because he
had to have help. It is thus that we remember our
Heavenly Friend. It is terribly easy to forget God. It is
especially easy if "the sea of life is smooth and every moment jewelled with a joy." It is deadly easy if we are
prosperous, if our health is good, if everything is coming to us right side up. Therefore, the days of greatest
spiritual power for the church are not those days when
the church is on easy street. It is the blood of the
martyrs that has been the seed of the church through
the years. It is when life gets hard that we most often
turn to God. When, therefore, this man found himself
up against it, he thought of his friend as one who was
willing and able to help him. Even so, many of us,

when we get up against it, think of God as one who is willing and able to help us.

But there was a second step that this host had to take, or the reality of his friend and his ability and willingness to help him would have come to nothing. He must give that friend a chance. Some years ago there was a self-important woman in a certain church who became ill. She was ill for several weeks, and during all that time her minister did not pay her a single visit. As soon as she had sufficiently recovered, she hurried to the pastor's study to tell him how terribly he had treated her and to ask for her church certificate.

"Did your physician come to see you?" the minister asked.

"Certainly he did."

"How did that come about?"

"Why," she answered, "I sent for him."

"Why did you not send for me?" he asked. "You did not tell me. Nobody else told me. How did you expect me to come to see you when you did not give me a chance?" That is the way we sometimes treat the pastor. Sadder still, that is the way we sometimes treat God.

A promise, whether human or divine, must be claimed. Years ago, as a young chap, I was eager to go to college but was very short of funds. Therefore I took a long chance and made application for a scholarship to Harvard University. One night I went over to the little village post office for the mail. There was only one letter. I saw that the letter was addressed to me. When I opened it, it read like this: "Your application for a scholarship to Harvard University has been favorably considered. Please report at Lower Massachusetts Hall, September 28 at ten A.M."

Now there were three courses I could have taken about that matter. I could have looked at that letter with wistful eyes and said: "It is a wonderful promise but entirely too good to be true. Besides, if I should go to Cambridge, I would have to borrow the money on which to go. Therefore, if when I arrived they should fail to make their promise good, I would certainly be in a mess. So the only thing to do is to tear up the letter and forget about it."

A second course I might have taken would have been to have said: "Well, I am the first man from my backwoods village that ever sought to enter Harvard. They are not going to pass up the opportunity of receiving a man from a village from which no student has come since the morning stars sang together. Therefore they will give me the scholarship if I meet the conditions, or they will give it to me if I do not meet the conditions."

But the course I took was this: With laughter fairly shaking my soul, I said to myself, "I will be there if I am not dead. On September 28 at ten o'clock, I am going to walk into Lower Massachusetts Hall with this letter in my hand. If those Yankees do not keep their promise, it will go hard with their word." Thus acting, I received the scholarship.

This embarrassed host acted with a like wisdom. He went to his friend. He told him in simple language

15

what he wanted. He did not make an oration. He did not deliver a speech. He simply stated the case, and then he gave his friend time to act. Jesus recognized the fact that often there are delays in answers to prayer. Sometimes these delays are for reasons that we ourselves can understand, sometimes for reasons known only to God. But this man stood at the door of his friend and waited. This he did for two good reasons. First, he waited because he had to have the bread. Second, he waited because he was sure that the bread would be given.

It so happens that I love the mountains. I especially love to see a sunrise in the mountains. Suppose you were to tell me that if I should make my way to a certain peak, promptly at six o'clock in the morning, I would be privileged to see heaven opened by the glory of a sunrise. Suppose further I should work my way to that peak and be standing there with my eyes on my watch at the appointed hour. Suppose that six o'clock came, but no sunrise. What would I do then? Turn away and say, "The sun is not going to rise today"? No, I would say one of two things. I would say, "Maybe my watch is wrong, or maybe my friend has made a mistake. But there is one thing that is absolutely sure: the sun is going to rise sometime." Even so, I ought to be sure that if I keep my place upon my watchtower, the Sun of Righteousness will also rise upon me with healing in his beams. We have to give our friend a chance.

Now, when this man gave his friend a chance, what

happened? I met him on his way back home. He had a new spring in his step and a new lilt in his voice. I said, "Did you get the three loaves for which you asked?" He answered, "I do not know. I have not counted them yet. But I got what I needed, I am sure of that." Not only did he get all the bread he needed, but he got a new confidence in his friend and a new love for him. Not only that, he got a new capacity to help. So it is with all who really pray. "He will rise and give him as many as he needeth."

III

What are your needs? I do not know. Perhaps you do not know. But there is one who does, and that is God. Whatever those needs may be, of this I am sure, he stands ready to meet them. There are certain basic needs that we all have in common. These God stands ready to meet for every one of us.

First, if we pray, we can receive God's pardoning grace and mercy. We all need to have said to us what Jesus said to some friends centuries ago, friends who had failed him miserably. He said, "Rise up, let us be going." We need that pardon that means the restoration of a fellowship.

We need the conviction that our Lord has run his arm through ours in his forgiving love and that he walks with us as if we had never failed him. That we can have in answer to prayer.

Second, prayer gives courage. It gives an inner serenity and poise to face life unafraid. Here is a word that comes out of a long gone past: "I sought the Lord, and he heard me, and delivered me from all my fears." These words are just as fresh at this moment as when they were uttered. They have the dewdrops of an eternal morning upon them. Of what this ancient psalmist was afraid we do not know. He may have been afraid of the passing of the springtime and the oncoming of the loneliness of the autumn days. He may have been afraid of the loss of his wealth, or of the loss of his health. He may have been afraid of the fact that sin had taken one he loved into its destroying hands and was tearing his soul to bits. But whatever his fear, when he brought those fears into the presence of God, they vanished like mist before the sunrise.

That is not mere theory. That is experience. Perhaps it is your experience. I can humbly say that it is my own experience. I have looked forward to ordeals that made me desperately afraid. I have found myself in the midst of those ordeals with a courage and a serenity that were a surprise to my own heart.

I am sure that I found that courage because I had prayed. Thus prayer brings to those who pray a strength that they could not have otherwise. It is true both in scripture and in experience that "they that wait upon the Lord shall renew their strength."

Here is a man strong by nature, but he is in a situation that is desperately hard. He is on board an ancient sailing vessel that is manned by a pagan crew. That vessel has been pounded by the fists of a storm for nearly fourteen days. So terrific has been that pounding that the ship is now going to pieces. Not only so, but every man on board, both passengers and crew, is going to pieces also. There is only one exception; that is a man named Paul. Moffatt's translation reads, "After long abstinence Paul stood up in the midst of them." Paul stood up. I like that. When others were going to pieces, Paul stood up and said, "Be of good cheer . . . for there stood by me this night the angel of God, whose I am, and whom I serve, saying, 'Fear not, Paul; thou must be brought before Caesar: and lo, God hath given thee all them that sail with thee.' " Paul found strength for himself and strength to save others because he prayed.

This has been the experience of countless others. Years ago I stood with others facing a situation that looked utterly hopeless. Then one daring man, as did Paul, stood up. "I love to get in a hard place for my Lord," he affirmed with humble confidence. "I love to get in a place that is so hard that there is no chance to get through without I get down on both hands and knees and crawl through to God." It sounds a bit crude, but it is a crudeness akin to that of John Bunyan. I will say this further, that through that one believing man God wrought a victory that is still one of the bright spots in my ministry. Now it strikes me that internationally, nationally, and individually we have reached that hard place, that place that is so hard that there is no chance to get through without we get down on both hands and knees and crawl through to God. Therefore may the Lord teach us to pray.

II

ENJOYING RELIGION

*"Again, the kingdom of heaven is like unto
a treasure hid in a field; the which when a
man hath found, he hideth, and for joy thereof
goeth and selleth all that he hath, and buyeth
that field."*

MATTHEW 13:44

"AND FOR JOY THEREOF." THAT IS A STRIKING PHRASE.
Here is a man at whom his neighbors must have
looked with bewildered and yet wistful eyes. "He is so
different," they said to one another. "He is different from
us. He is different from his former self. When I saw him
this morning as he was going to his work in the field of
another man, he certainly did not impress me as one who
was on his way to a new day of high adventure. He
rather looked as if he were only going to the drab
monotony of just another day. But now look at him. He
is utterly different. He has been completely transformed."

Not only so, but what is stranger still, he is absurdly
joyous while seemingly reducing himself to poverty.

20

Having sold his very all, he is now pushing every penny of his wealth over the counter into the hands of a real estate dealer. He is paying all that he has in return for the field that he used to work. Perhaps in the mind of his neighbors he is paying far more than the field is worth. But, however that may be, he is gladly paying his all as if convinced that the owner is doing him a favor by thus relieving him of his money. He seems to regard what looks like a great sacrifice as in reality a priceless privilege. "And for joy thereof [he] goeth and selleth all that he hath, and buyeth that field."

I

What does Jesus mean? He is telling us that finding the kingdom and entering into it, while costly, is a source of joy. It is a source of supreme joy. Of course, all of us do not believe this. We still feel that, while religion is good for the afterlife, it is rather a burden for the life that now is. It is something that we must put through somehow, but it is more a weight than wings. It is something to be endured rather than to be enjoyed. But Jesus affirms that vital religion is a source of supreme joy.

This conviction is shared by the writers of both the Old and New Testaments. When we turn even to the Old Testament, where there is much that is gloomy and forbidding, we find that this note of joy is upon the lips of almost all the saints. Of course, we meet there some very pious people who did not enjoy their religion. There were some who were bored by it even as we. There were some who said, "What a weariness it is." They had to deal with so many prohibitions, so many petty laws. But some found that even these need not be altogether burdensome. We hear one of the psalmists declaring, "Thy statues have been my songs in the house of my pilgrimage." In fact, we find in the Psalms, the amazing hymnbook of the Jews, reflected almost every mood of the human soul. If we feel inclined to sob, we meet here those who will share our sorrow. But the predominant note of the book is one of joy. Here we find life set to music.

Take for instance the author of the thirty-fourth psalm. He was a man who at one time had been dogged by tormenting fears. I do not know what he was afraid of. He may have been afraid that some ugly sin of his yesterday might reach out of the past to grip and to destroy him. He may have been afraid of tomorrow. Whatever were his fears, he brought them before God. "I sought the Lord," he sings, "and he heard me." So what? "And delivered me from all my fears." Thus set free, he went forth in the comfort and peace of the fellowship of God.

Naturally his story was too good to keep. He had to tell it to his needy fellows. He knew some whose faces had become mantled with a settled gloom. The light had gone out of their eyes. So he told them his own experience, with the result that they too found help. "They looked unto him, and were lightened: and their faces were not ashamed."

In the fortieth psalm we meet another man who had found life hard and disappointing. He had lived, not in the light, but in the darkness of a spiritual dungeon. His dungeon was a miry and noisome place where life was utterly tragic. But he tells us that he waited patiently for the Lord and that the Lord inclined unto him and heard him. Indeed he brought him up out of the horrible pit and out of the miry clay and set his feet upon a rock and established his going. Naturally this experience had put a new song in the man's mouth, a song of joy and praise. Thus, over and over, do these psalms set life to music. They were written by men who had found in their religion a source of supreme joy.

When we turn to the New Testament, we find this note of joy intensified. This is the case in spite of the fact that the New Testament, in all good sense, should have been vastly depressing. It tells of the grimmest tragedy that was ever enacted upon this planet. It tells how Incarnate Goodness came to live among us and how we men knew nothing better to do with him than to crown him with a crown of thorns and hang him on a cross. But in spite of this, the New Testament is not a depressing book, but the most joyous ever written. This is the case because at the center of the book lives the most joyous of men.

We need to bear in mind that Jesus, in spite of the cross, yes, and because of the cross, was the most sunny soul that ever looked out upon this world. Does not the writer to the Hebrews tell us that he was anointed with the oil of gladness above his fellows? Again and again he had upon his lips this bracing word, "Be of good cheer." In the last prayer with his friends he prayed that the joy that was his might be theirs. When, at their last meal together, he took the cup that was the symbol of life poured out, he took it with thanksgiving. Then he went out to Gethsemane and to the cross with a song on his lips. "When they had sung an hymn, they went out."

Now this prayer that Jesus prayed, that the joy that was his might belong to his friends, was answered. To be convinced of this, it is only necessary to turn almost at random to the book of Acts or to the epistles. Here we meet whole groups of people whose faces are so full of sunshine, whose lips are so full of song, that it makes us wistful even to look at them across the years. They themselves find it hard to credit their own good fortune. As the saints of the Bible are a sunny lot, so have they been through the centuries. So they are still. I have met such in all my congregations. These committed folks, while differing in many respects, have in common a deep and abiding joy.

Nor is this joy a mere hothouse plant. Trusting souls do not have to be in favorable circumstances in order to sing. On the contrary, it would seem that their joy reaches its supreme height in times of gloom and darkness; that the blacker the night, the more radiant the light in their souls. Here for instance are two men, Peter and John, who have just undergone a shameful ordeal. They have been whipped like slaves. Yet as they go from this experience, they go with a sparkle in their eyes and a spring in their steps, as if they had just been decorated for valor. "Rejoicing that they were counted worthy to suffer shame for his name."

Here are two others. It is midnight and they are in jail. Not only are they in jail, but they are in the inner prison with their feet fast in the stocks. Their backs are gashed and bleeding. They, too, have been publicly whipped. But though it is midnight according to the calendar and midnight in their fortunes, in their hearts it is bright morning. They are so joyous that they give a concert. They cannot help singing and praying. Therefore it is not too amazing that the prison doors opened and that the locked door of the jailer's heart opened as well. He almost had to welcome as Lord one who could give songs in the night.

This is experienced today by those who have committed themselves to the Lord, regardless of their circumstances. I went recently to see a young woman who had been made an utter physical wreck by an automobile accident. She was blinded in both eyes. She was paralyzed from her shoulders down. Knowing in advance her pathetic plight, I prepared myself to say a few words of comfort. But when I was introduced, the brightness of her face and the lilt of her voice put me to silence. Her evident and abounding joy amazed me. My amazement was greater still after the nurse whispered to me, "She is in great agony every moment of her waking existence." The patient overheard this, and her face became even brighter. Then she said, "You know, as I lie here and suffer, I catch myself wishing that I might bear the pain of others." Her presence was as refreshing as a breath from snowy mountains on a sultry day. This, then, is fact—vital religion is a source of deep and abiding joy—regardless of circumstances.

II

Why is this man so joyous?

Well, is it not because he has secured the prize that he coveted at a bargain. Bargain counter saints are seldom distinguished by their joy. If a cheap religion brought joy, many today would be singing instead of merely being bored. Certainly many of us are giving to the Lord that which costs us nothing. But we are not pleased with our bargain. This is the case because a cheap religion is one that never satisfies either God or man.

This man is not only not joyous because he is getting the prize at a bargain. He is rather joyous because it is costing him his very all. That is constantly the case. In order to enter the kingdom, we must make an unconditional surrender. That is the door, and there is no other door. Our Lord is not asking for our tears or for our prayers or for our money or for our work first of all. He is asking for us. He is asking for a dedicated life. If we give that, we enter the kingdom. If we do not give that, the door is automatically shut in our faces.

Not only is dedication the door of entrance; it is also the life. When Paul met Jesus on the way from Jerusalem to Damascus, he made an unconditional surrender. He tells his own experience in these words, "I was not disobedient unto the heavenly vision." He died to himself that day. But one dying was not enough. According to his own testimony he died daily. It was by this daily dying that he passed from the "these things" of his conversion to the "those things" of that deeper and richer experience that enabled him to say: "I am crucified with Christ: nevertheless I live; yet not I, but Christ liveth in me."

It is through dedication, then, that we enter the kingdom. It is through dedication that we come really to know Jesus Christ. He said, "If any man will do his will, he shall know." Thus as we come to know him, he

26

takes captive our hearts. He enables us to begin then and there to live the life of love.

Now, it is a fact that we are always glad to work or to give to any person or to any cause that we deeply love. Take work for instance. My father was a farmer. He was a farmer from choice. He loved farming. He loved the cultivation of the soil. He loved to see things grow. I, on the contrary, had no such taste. I used to stand and look over that farm and say to myself: "I do not know what I will do when I am grown, but I know what I am not going to do. I am not going to farm." Therefore I was a bit allergic to the kind of work in which my father had real delight.

It is easy to work and to sacrifice for a person that one loves. When Ruth was turning her back upon her native land and her own people, she did not do so grudgingly. She did so eagerly because of the larger love that had come into her life. Therefore she clung to Naomi, saying: "Intreat me not to leave thee, or to return from following after thee: for whither thou goest, I will go; and where thou lodgest, I will lodge: thy people shall be my people, and thy God my God. Where thou diest, will I die, and there will I be buried." She was eager because she cared.

Here Paul is sharing with us a very rich experience through which he has just passed. "While visiting a certain church," he tells us, "I was literally besieged by beggars. They fairly clung to me and would not take no for an answer." For what were these persistent folks begging? They were begging for the privilege of making a donation. They were begging for the privilege of taking part in the collection. Why was this case? Not be-

27

cause they were rich—they were very poor. It was the case because "they had first given themselves to the Lord." Having dedicated their own lives, they were glad to dedicate their substance also.

It is this dedication of self that makes all giving, all living, a joy. Now and then I hear some boast of the sacrifices that they have made. I seldom hear such boasting that I see any mark of real sacrifice. Those who have given their all do not look upon it as a sacrifice but as a privilege. Here is a man, a philosopher, a scholar, a musician, a theologian, a physician. He seems to have almost every gift. He has given up a career in his native land to live in the most vicious climate in the world, equatorial Africa. He is living there amidst ignorance and disease. The jungle has to be fought every single day. His wife cannot live with him because the climate is so deadly. But when certain newspaper reporters asked Albert Schweitzer about his sacrifice, he answered, "I have never made any. I have had the joy of doing good." Joy follows on the heels of dedication to God as naturally as night follows the day.

III

How then shall we know this joy?

We are not going to find it by saying to ourselves, "Go to now, I am going to have a good time." The rich farmer knew that he ought to be having a better time than he was having. Therefore he sought to arouse his sluggish soul to gladness by telling it to eat, drink, and be merry. But after all his prodding he was just as wretched as he had been before. Did you ever get in a hurry to go to sleep? If so you discovered that the more you hurried the wider awake you became. So it is with those who seek joy as an end. About the most restless and wretched people we meet are those whose one purpose in life is to have a good time.

If we are not to find this joy by seeking it as an end, no more do we find it by seeking its opposite. There are those who seem to feel that they really ought not to enjoy their religion. They are convinced that the more miserable they make themselves, the more Christian they are likely to be. I am thinking of a friend who seems to have a martyr complex. He clings to the gloom as a vine to old ruins. He seems to regard his wretchedness as a positive virtue. But of course he is wrong. Joy is more than a privilege; it is a positive duty. "The joy of the Lord is your strength." It is your strength for vital Christian living. It is your strength for resisting temptation. It is your strength for winning others. Few, I think, are won to Christ by people whose faces "do cream and mantle like a standing pond." We do not find joy by seeking its opposite.

How then, I repeat, shall we find this joy? We shall find it as all the saints have found it, by the giving of self. Jesus found his joy in that fashion. He said, "My yoke is easy." What was his yoke? It was the yoke of a life perfectly dedicated to God. "My food is to do the will of Him who sent me, and to accomplish his work." We therefore find joy not by seeking it as an end nor by seeking its opposite. We rather find it by seeking first the kingdom of God and his righteousness. Having put him first, whatever we have to do or suffer is transformed into privilege because we meet it in his fellowship.

Here then are two roads, the road of self-pleasing and the road of self-giving. Here is a man whose radiant face glows upon us across the far spaces of the years like a star. His name was Joseph. But he so completely gave himself that his name was changed, and he came to be called Son of Encouragement. Everybody felt the spell of the moral and spiritual beauty of Barnabas. This was surely true of a fellow churchman named Ananias. But though desiring the prize, he was unwilling to pay the price of self-giving. Therefore, though I do not claim fully to understand his story, this I do know—that he did not find the life that he desired. He found only death. That is a universal experience.

> She built herself a little house
>   All walled around with pride,
> Took Prudence for her servant
>   And shut herself inside.
>
> She pulled her blinds down tight as tight
>   When sorrow chanced to roam.
> Experience called; she sent down word
>   That she was not at home.
>
> Then wherefore should she now complain,
>   And wherefore should she sigh,
> If life and love and laughter
>   Have passed unseeing by?

Here is a man that took the opposite road:

ENJOYING RELIGION

O Joy that seekest me through pain,
  I cannot close my heart to Thee;
I trace the rainbow through the rain,
And feel the promise is not vain
  That morn shall tearless be.

O Cross that liftest up my head,
  I dare not ask to fly from Thee;
I lay in dust life's glory dead,
And from the ground there blossoms red
  Life that shall endless be.

"And for joy thereof [he] goeth and selleth all that he hath and buyeth that field." Thus he set his feet on the path to the fullness of joy.

III

SO MUCH FOR SO LITTLE

"So the last shall be first, and the first last."

MATTHEW 20:16

THIS IS THE SPEAR POINT OF THE GRIPPING STORY THAT Jesus has just told. Of course, he does not mean that every man who is first is going to be last, nor that every man who is last is to be first. He only means that this sometimes happens. Or, as he puts it at the beginning of the story, "Many that are first shall be last, and the last shall be first."

There is little doubt that every man present when Jesus told this unique story listened to it with keenest interest and attention. Some were doubtless shocked by the seeming unfairness of it. Others who were handicapped and who were coming close to the sunset without much to show for their day listened eagerly because it brought a gleam of hope. Perhaps these felt that it was far too good to be true, but in spite of this fact, it made their gloomy day a bit brighter.

SO MUCH FOR SO LITTLE

I

Look at the story. It tells of an eccentric landlord who hired laborers for his vineyard and paid them off in a very surprising fashion. It is striking also that this landlord hired any man who was willing to work, regardless of the lateness of the hour.

1. Look first at the laborers. They fall naturally into three groups.

a) There were those sons of good fortune who succeeded in making contact with an employer in the early morning. These men naturally had bargaining powers that their belated fellows did not have. They could say to the owner of the vineyard. "What will you pay for a day's work?" When he answered, "I will pay each of you a dollar a day," that was satisfactory. Having thus reached an agreement, these men went into the vineyard for a full day's work.

b) The second group was made up of those who were hired at nine, twelve, and three o'clock. These did not have the same bargaining powers as their more fortunate fellows who found employment at the beginning of the day. Their employer offered them no fixed wages. He only pledged himself to give them a square deal. Therefore, they went into the vineyard trusting this promise: "Whatsoever is right, I will pay you."

c) The third group, and the one which holds the center of the stage, is made up of those hired about five o'clock. When the landlord went out at this late hour and found these still without work, he questioned them, "Why stand ye here all the day idle or workless?" In reply these depressed and discouraged men gave an honest answer, "We are workless because nobody has hired us. Our idleness is not our fault, but our misfortune." Then said the landlord, "Go ye also into the vineyard." He gave them no promise of reward, only a command. It speaks volumes, therefore, for their eagerness that they took this, their first opportunity. They hurried to earn even the pitiful pittance that they were sure would be paid them for working only one twelfth of a day.

2. Then, one hour later, came the pay-off. Those who had come last into the vineyard were paid first. That is what got this employer into trouble. If he had just paid the full-time men first, they would have gone home without knowing of the good fortune of the latecomers. But he paid the five o'clock men first. Not only so, but to their great joy he paid them a full day's wages. What a burden that lifted! No child emptying his full stocking on Christmas morning could find greater gladness than these found in the amazing generosity of their employer.

Naturally, such generosity awakened the expectations of the others. This was especially true of those who had worked for twelve full hours. They knew that if their employer was thus generous to them they would receive wages not for one day, but for twelve. When, therefore, they received only that for which they had agreed, they were indignant. They appointed a spokesman, it would seem, who presented their cause to the landlord. What was their complaint? Not that they had been cheated, but that others had been rewarded beyond their deserts. "Thou hast made them equal unto us."

Their employer answered wisely, "I do thee no wrong." Surely he is perfectly right. You cannot pos-

34

sibly wrong me by doing a favor to my neighbor. It would seem that in his indignation this full-time man had thrown down his dollar, saying, "If you can't pay me more than that, I won't have anything." This is indicated by the fact that his employer said, "Take up that which is thine and go thy way. I will give unto this last as unto thee." "Thus," concludes Jesus, "the last shall be first, and the first last."

II

It is evident from this that our Lord's standard for measuring success is different from ours. It is well to remember that Jesus is not here teaching a lesson in economics. I think there is no doubt of his keen interest in the right of men to work and to work for an adequate wage. There is no surer sign of a sick social order than that men willing to work cannot do so. That "pursuit of happiness" guaranteed under the Declaration of Independence is impossible for the man who is without work. Yet any man who would conduct his business as did this ancient landlord would go broke. This is the case because an employee must put into the firm at least as much as he takes out or that firm will inevitably go on the rocks.

For this reason we tend to measure the worth of our fellows largely by the returns they make. For instance, a few years ago I stepped into the office of a newspaper to be greeted by this word that glared at me from the wall in boxcar letters: "Fifty-seven rules for making a success. First—deliver the goods! Second—it doesn't make any difference about the other fifty-six." There you have it.

During the days of the depression I heard the head of a large chemical company make this statement: "To-morrow, when I get to my office it will be crowded by men seeking employment. But most of them I cannot use because they are inefficient. This will be the case in spite of the fact that many of them are from our best American universities. This will be true in spite of the fact that some of them are from the best universities of Germany. But there is little use for one to be educated on the Rhine unless he can bring home the bacon." "Deliver the goods"—"bring home the bacon." That is the test.

But this story indicates that our Lord has rich rewards for those who do not, in the fullest sense, deliver the goods and who do not bring home the bacon. These men who had worked but one hour received a full day's wages not because they had really earned that much. They were rewarded not for what they had actually accomplished, but for what they would have accomplished had it been in their power. Their employer took the will for the deed. Browning must have had this in mind when the said, "It is not what man does, but what man would do that exalts him."

The fact that these five o'clock men had been jobless all day does not mean that they had been sitting in the shade having a good time. They had not been idle, but jobless. They had not only worked, but had done so under the most depressing and discouraging circumstances. They had worked by going from one market place to another in search of a job. They had worked dogged by fear, the fear that they would be rated as failures. Not only so, but they were tortured by the still greater fear that at the close of the day they would be asked for bread that they could not give. In addition they had worked with a sense of uselessness gnawing like a rat at their self-respect. There was a certain fairness, therefore, and vast kindness in their being paid more than they had earned.

This is constantly God's way. I am quite sure that the supreme ambition of David was to build a temple to the honor of his God. I daresay that it was because of this temple that he expected to live in the grateful hearts of his people. But while he was able to accomplish much, this dream never came true. When he reached the end of the journey, there was no temple in Jerusalem to perpetuate his memory. Therefore, he probably passed on with a deep sense of failure. But God said to him, "Whereas it was in thine heart to build me a house, thou didst well that it was in thine heart." That is, though David left no temple upon Mount Moriah, God gave him credit for such an achievement because of the temple that he had builded in his own heart.

This fact explains the enthusiasm of Jesus over the gift of the poor widow. "And Jesus sat over against the treasury, and beheld how the people cast money into the treasury: and many that were rich cast in much. And there came a certain poor widow and she threw in two mites, which make a farthing." At that, Jesus sprang to his feet with cheeks aglow. He could not wait until the service was over to say to his friends, "This poor widow has cast in more than all they which have cast into the treasury." This was the case not because of what she had given with her hand, but what she had given with her heart.

This should give hope to the handicapped. It should excite expectation in the hearts of those who feel that they are coming to the end of the journey with little to show for their struggles. I have known many of this kind. I am thinking now of a bright young chap in the Ozark Mountains who felt himself called to the ministry. He labored hard on his mountain farm to accumulate enough to enter college. At last the glad day came when he was on his way to the station to take the train. But his car was wrecked. His back was broken. He was confined to his bed not simply for days and weeks and months, but even years. At last, when he emerged from his torture chamber, his hopes of entering the ministry were dead. He had to take the only job that was offered, that of ferryman on the Osage River. This he did not in bitterness, but with a fine, high gallantry.

Here is a charming and high-spirited girl who had dedicated her life to the mission field. She was soon to be married to a choice young man who shared her dream, and they were going out to those distant fields together. But tragedy struck. Her brother, who had been the stay of the family, died. Then the mother. This left an invalid father and an imbecile brother. It therefore became necessary for this girl to give up her dream of working on far horizons. Life for her narrowed down to taking care of a whining old invalid and a stupid brother. At last these two passed into the sunset, but by that time spring had given place to summer, and summer to late autumn. The high-spirited girl was then the old maid of the village. But through it all she had been of a courageous, brave, and cheerful spirit.

Now I have an idea that the record of this young minister who was never privileged to preach a single sermon, and of this young woman who had to give up her dream of wifehood and of labor in the mission field is not going to be blank. I think our gracious Lord, who understands, is going to say to each of them, "Whereas it was in thine heart to do these great and romantic deeds for me, thou didst well that it is in thine heart."

III

But what is the test of what is in our hearts?

The fact that God judges us not by what we do but by what we would do is often very comforting. Some may even make an opiate of it. There are those who, being handicapped, feel that they can make their contribution by cheap alibis. They satisfy themselves by telling what they would do if they could. They tell how much they would give if they were as rich as some Croesus. They tell how faithfully they would work if they had the skill of some friend. Meantime they are doing nothing with the opportunities that are really theirs.

The test of what is in our hearts is what we do with what is actually in our hands. These five o'clock laborers were rewarded because they had done their best with the opportunities that were actually theirs. When their employer said, "Go also into the vineyard," they did not turn on him angrily and ask, "Why did you not employ us sooner?" No more did they say in self-pity, "It is too late now. What is the good of one twelfth of a day's wages anyway?" In spite of the fact that there seemed so little to be gained, they took what opportunity they had and made the best possible use of it.

We know that God credited David with the building of the temple, though he did not build it at all except in his heart. But how do we know that David really had it in his heart to build the temple? We know it because when he found that he could not build it, when he found that it would not be David's temple, instead of losing interest, he went just as far as he could toward building it. He did his best with what he had.

How do we know of the magnificent wealth that the poor widow had in her heart? Only in one way. By what she did with what was actually hers. Had she set out that morning to the temple leaving her two mites behind her, she would have had much to say for herself. She could have said, "There will be many rich people at the service today who will cast in handfuls of gold. I too would cast in a handful of gold if I had it, but since I have only a fraction of a cent, I will not embarrass myself by giving anything." But she won immortality by giving what was actually hers.

Take the young minister who had to turn aside from the pulpit to fill the prosaic job of ferryman. What indication is there that God is going to reward him for a success greater than he seems to have achieved? Here is the answer. Shut off from the privileges of preaching from the pulpit, he preached at his task day by day. The friend who told me his story said that there were no less than seventy men living in the neighboring mountains who had been won to Christ by the personal appeal of this man who talked to them as he ferried them across the river.

SO MUCH FOR SO LITTLE

Here, then, is this searching and comforting fact: God judges us by what is in our hearts. But the test of what is in our hearts is what we do with that which we have in our hands. This puts us all on an equal footing. The greatly gifted have no better chance than those of meager gifts. The handicapped have the same opportunity as the highly privileged. This fact makes this test at once very searching and very conforting.

It is very searching for those who are greatly gifted. It is easy for the man of great gifts to be contented with his big returns, even when he has done far less than his best. God is not going to ask us how much we have done but how faithfully we have worked.

This is full of hope for the handicapped. I meet so many who have failed to realize their dreams. On the campus of a certain American college there is a monument to a former pupil which reads in part: "To the memory of Jim . . . , died in France saving the life of a comrade." Then this last in small letters: "He played four years on the scrubs." What a story that tells! Of course, we honor the men who make the first team. Were I playing, I should like to become an All-American. But what of men like Jim who, failing to make first or second team, can still play with the scrubs for long years and never grow either discouraged or sour? Beyond a doubt it was his willingness to play his best on a scrub team that helped him to play the best in later years on the field of battle. Surely such heroic souls shall have their reward. "So the last shall be first."

IV

WITHOUT LIMIT

"Until seventy times seven ..."

MATTHEW 18:22

WHILE THIS WHOLE STORY IS OUR SUBJECT, I AM CALL-
ing your special attention to these words: "Until
seventy times seven." Simon Peter has come to Jesus
with a question. In this question he has set an exceedingly high standard. He was conscious of the fact, and
if you do not think he was correct examine your own
heart. "How often," he asked, "shall my brother sin
against me and I forgive him? Until seven times?" Some
of us cannot manage even once. So Simon was setting
the standard very high. But Jesus did not commend
him. He said, "I say not unto thee, until seven times:
but until seventy times seven."

By this Jesus did not mean that we are to forgive four
hundred and ninety times and then stop. He rather
meant that we are constantly to exercise a forgiving
spirit. We are to forgive without limit. Forgiveness is
to flow from our hearts as constantly as water from a
brimming spring, as constantly as light comes from the

sun. It is a standard so high that it seems entirely impossible. The one bright spot in it is this: If Jesus expects so much of us, he will not give less to us. He will forgive us without limit.

I

This unlimited forgiveness is to be exercised toward all the cranky folks with whom we have to deal. Let us look at a few of these.

1. There are the folks who differ from us. Of course, everybody ought to be just like us. They ought to belong to our nation and to be of our color. But God has seen fit to make them different. Therefore we have a tendency to look critically at them and to blame them for being what they are. Of course, we cannot help realizing that to blame any man for being the color that the Lord made him is to reflect on God rather than on the man himself. But in spite of this we still find it hard to forgive folks for differing from us in color or race.

Then there are those who differ socially and economically. There are some who have not had our educational opportunities. They do not have as flourishing a family tree as ours. They do not have as good bank accounts. They do not drive as good cars. Therefore they are naturally beneath us, and we have a right to look down on them. Even more we have a right to look askance at those who have a better social position than we, or who drive better cars and have bigger bank accounts. We resent the fact that they got all the breaks, or that they resorted to practices to which we were too good to resort. We say of them, as Mary did of her rival to whom she had lost her favorite beau,

"I could have kept him if I had cheapened myself as Nancy did."

We also resent those who differ from us in their opinions and convictions. What we believe about political issues, what we believe on the liquor question, is necessarily right. Years ago when we were having a hard wet and dry fight in the city where I was pastor, a member of my congregation, a most ardent dry, told me of one of our officials who had taken the opposite side. So indignant was he against this man that he declared that he hoped every child of his would become a drunkard. John, who became the beloved apostle, was anything but a bad man, yet at one stage of his life he found it easier to tolerate demons than to tolerate a brother who while casting out demons refused to belong to this particular group.

We also find it hard to forgive those who refuse to share our prejudices and our hates. About the first violent opposition that Jesus met was because of his refusal to share the hates and prejudices of his native village. He told those villagers that there had been something so good about a woman in the land of Jezebel that God had chosen her to board his prophet Elijah. He told them further that though there had been many lepers in Israel during the days of Elisha, not one of them had had the faith to be cured. Such a faith had been possessed only by an outsider named Naaman. At this they became so enraged that Jesus barely escaped being mobbed. It is easy to hate those who are different.

2. We find it easy to resent those who do not accord us the consideration that we feel we deserve. Had you stepped onto the streets of Shushan some 2,500 years

44

ago, you would not have been on those streets fifteen minutes before somebody would have told you about Haman. Haman was a self-made man. He was the most powerful man in the Persian empire. So powerful was he that when he appeared on the streets everybody bowed low, that is, everybody except one stubborn Jew named Mordecai. But his refusal to bow so enraged Haman that he forgot all those who did bow to give the remainder of his days to seeking revenge against this man. So intense became his hatred that it ended by hanging Haman on his own gallows, as hate has a way of doing.

Years ago I knew a minister who was very popular in the church where he was serving. Whenever he took a pinch of snuff everybody sneezed. Then he went to another church in a distant state. Naturally he wanted to begin where he left off. He expected those new people to say, "He that has turned the world upside down has come here also." But they failed to say it. On the contrary, when he spilled a whole box of snuff in that situation nobody sneezed. Naturally he was soon eager to go on to greener pastures.

3. A third group that we find it hard to forgive is those who have done us positive wrong. They have borrowed money that they have refused to repay. They have beaten us out of our part of the estate. They have spoken evil against us. Possibly they have actually lied on us. What is worse still, they have wronged one whom we love. There is no mistaking the fact that they have done us dirt. Therefore we often feel that we have a right to resent and to get even with them.

4. Then there are the folks whom we have wronged,

whose wrongs we refuse to set right. This, I think, is the sharpest test of our forgiving spirit. This is the case because if we wrong anybody and refuse to apologize, we have to give ourselves a reason for such refusal. In seeking a reason we look for the worst in the one whom we have wronged instead of the best. By thus looking for the worst we never fail to find it. Having found it we succeed in convincing ourselves that they deserve our ill treatment and our resulting hate. I think, therefore, that there is nobody that we find it harder to forgive than the man whom we have wronged if we refuse so far as in us lies to right that wrong.

II

Why are we to forgive?

1. We are to forgive because hate is so deadly. It works untold injury upon the hated. There is no measuring the cost of hate among the nations. There is no measuring its cost to churches and to families. It has been deadly to the individual. When the Count of Monte Cristo escaped from prison, he tracked down those who had wronged him. He hung upon their steps like an avenging bloodhound. It is terrible to be the victim of a hate like that.

But if it is terrible to be the victim of hate like that, it is still more terrible to be the possessor of such hate. Cruel as are the wrongs that hate has inflicted upon the hated, it always strikes the most deadly blows at the hater. Of all the emotions that tear personality into shreds and tatters, there is none equal to hate. It is a poison to the body, it is a poison to the mind, it is a poison to the soul. We ought to be rid of hate because hate means hell.

2. We must be willing to forgive in order to receive the forgiveness of God. Jesus promised forgiveness only on one condition, that we be willing to forgive. "If ye forgive men their trespasses, your heavenly father will also forgive you." But we cannot be forgiven on any other terms. Again he said, "and when ye stand praying, forgive, if ye have ought against any: that your Father also which is in heaven may forgive you your trespasses." God is eager to forgive. He is extending his forgiveness in both his loving hands, but it is utterly impossible for us to receive that forgiveness unless we are willing to forgive.

This is not the case because God is vindictive. It is the case because of what forgiveness means. God can no more forgive the unforgiving than he can make death to be life at one and the same time. When God forgives us, he takes us back into his confidence and into his fellowship. By thus walking with us he changes us. We become partakers of the divine nature. He gives us a new heart and a new life. But not even God can give us what is new if we insist on clinging to what is old. Therefore we must forgive, or we can never know the forgiveness of God.

III

But how can we forgive?

1. Our gratitude ought to help us. God has been so good in forgiving us that we ought to find it possible to forgive others. Look at this story. Here is a man who

came into the presence of his king burdened by an unpayable debt, ten thousand talents. Nobody had that much money. When, therefore, the king, to save himself from losing all that was due him, ordered the man and his wife and his children and all he had to be sold, the poor chap had nothing to offer but a plea for mercy. "Have patience with me and I will pay thee all." At that the king, out of sheer pity, not only loosed him but forgave him his debt.

Now I was waiting just outside the door for this desperate friend of mine. When he came out, I saw at once that he was utterly transformed. His face looked like it had a sunrise behind it. "Whatever happened?" I asked.

"The impossible," he answered. "The king not only forgave me the debt but he set me free." But as we went arm in arm down the street I looked into that once radiant face to see that it had suddenly become black with night. Nor did I have to wait long to learn the reason. My once glad friend was gripping a white-faced chap by the throat and saying, "Pay me that hundred pence you owe me." Then when the poor fellow prayed exactly the same prayer that he himself had offered a few moments ago, instead of saying, "Forget it. I have just been forgiven an impossible debt," he had him cast in the prison. Naturally, he himself was cast into prison also, the prison of his own hate. He should have forgiven out of sheer gratitude.

2. Then our sense of need ought to lead us to forgive. If we have never sinned, then we do not need forgiveness. But since as sinners we need forgiveness, then we

48

ought to be willing to forgive others. A preacher of the very deep South told me a story the other day that warmed my heart. Into his church one Sunday morning there came a Negro man. A young usher showed the visitor to a pew. Since this happened to be a Communion Sunday, at the proper time he went forward with the Negro to take Communion. As ill fortune would have it, the next night was the meeting of the official board. The minister said that the atmosphere was very tense. Hardly had they got through the order of business when one red-faced chap sprang to his feet and said, "If anything like that ever occurs again, you may include me out."

But before the meeting ended in a free-for-all, as seemed threatened, the chairman had the wisdom to turn to the young usher and ask, "Why did you let that Negro into our church?"

"Well," he answered modestly, "I thought the very fact that he came to church indicated that he might be a Christian. I knew that if he was a Christian when he died he would go to heaven. I did not know but that when he got there God might make him an usher. Therefore, because I wanted him to let me in if he should be an usher, I let him in."

Our own sense of need ought to help us to forgive.

3. Perhaps our greatest help in forgiving is to act as if we had already forgiven. Jesus put it this way, "Bless them that curse you, and pray for them which despitefully use you." At first we may pray for our enemies when our hearts do not seem to be in our prayers, but if we persist in acting toward the man whom we do not like as if we liked him, the chances are

a thousand to one that we shall come to like him. This will be the case for one reason because as we do this our enemy will come to like us. That will make all the difference since there is nothing like love to win love from others.

Had I heard Jesus say to those ten lepers, "Go show yourselves to the priest," I think I would have felt a slight resentment. I should have said, "What in the world is he saying that for? They are to show themselves to the priest after they are cured, not before." But the lepers had faith enough in Jesus to believe that he was not sending them on a fool's errand. So they set out to see the priest, and it came to pass that as they went they were all cleansed. Even so, by acting as if we had really forgiven, we give God a chance. Into our hostile hearts will come his Spirit of love and of good will. The impossible is always possible to the man who obeys.

Here then is a road that we all must travel if we are to be Christians. We must all forgive. We ought to do so eagerly. Believe me, there is nothing in all the world more deadly than hate. There is nothing more rewarding than to forgive. Forgiveness is twice blessed. It blesses both him that gives and him that takes. When the patriarchs sold Joseph into slavery, they had every reason to believe that his pathway would end in the oblivion of a slave pen. This in all probability would have happened but for one reason. Joseph, though hated, refused to hate. He met his tragic wrong within the will of God. He realized that God had suffered in that wrong even more than he himself had suffered. So he said years later to his cringing brothers, "Ye thought evil against me; but God meant it unto good." By thus exercising a forgiving spirit toward these brothers, he saved both them and himself as well. Not only so, but he made it possible for the road that was expected to end in oblivion to end in a palace on the Nile, and in an immortality of usefulness.

Therefore let us forgive, not simply until seven times, but unto seventy times seven—that is, without limit.

V

IN THE NAME OF SENSE

"Which of you, intending to build a tower,
sitteth not down first, and counteth the cost?"

LUKE 14:28

JESUS WAS HERE FACING A GREAT CROWD. THOSE PEOPLE
had come to him because they were deeply interested in him and in his message. Among them there must
have been scores, perhaps hundreds, who were looking wistfully in his direction, half persuaded to cast
their lot in with him and become disciples. But Jesus,
instead of giving them a sales talk to break down their
remaining resistance, instead of seeking to high-pressure
them into an immediate decision, seems to have done
the very opposite. He doused them with this dash of
cold water: "Which of you, intending to build a tower,
sitteth not down first, and counteth the cost?" It would
seem as if he were uttering a word of cowardly caution,
as if he were saying: "Do not start anything unless you
are sure that you can see it through. Never go to bat
unless you are certain that you can hit a home run."
I confess that such a word from such a man seems to be
quite shocking.

52

IN THE NAME OF SENSE

I

What does Jesus mean by this parable that we call Counting the Cost? What is he saying to us?

We may be sure that he is uttering no word of cowardly caution. Had such been the case, Jesus would have been speaking out of character. Our Lord was not a cautious man. He was so lacking in caution that he became a storm center wherever he went. He was so lacking in caution that when he preached his first sermon in his home church, he changed an eager congregation into a bloodthirsty mob. He was so lacking in caution that he alienated from him the strong religious leaders who seemingly might have done most to make his cause victorious. He was so lacking in caution that he was done to death when he was in his early thirties.

Not only did Jesus practice what he preached, but he preached what he practiced. Being a daring man, he never urged caution upon others. In fact some of his sharpest rebukes were against those who were too cautious to act. He told of a man gifted with a talent who ended in the ashcan of worthless things. This was the case not because he squandered his talent but because he was too cautious and too cowardly to use it. "I was afraid," says the epitaph upon the buried possibilities of this man. Here as elsewhere Jesus warns against cowardice and caution.

As our Lord rebuked those who were too cautious, even so he gave unstinted praise to those who threw caution to the winds and acted with abandon. He declared that it was the violent who entered into the kingdom. At a dinner party one day he rose in indignant defense of a woman who had squandered enough perfume in one single act of devotion to have served for perhaps a hundred such acts. Naturally Judas and his friends were indignant. They thought the deed an ugly bit of waste. But Jesus declared that it was beautiful. In fact he said that it was so beautiful that her story would walk hand in hand with his own across all the centuries.

If Jesus is not here urging us to caution, what is he urging? In my opinion he is speaking a word in the name of common sense. He is eager that we make a choice, but he is not satisfied with that choice unless it is an intelligent choice. He is saying to us with the prophet, "Come, let us reason together." He longs that every one of us shall say with the psalmist, "I thought . . . and I turned." The man who refuses to think is generally the man who refuses to turn. But to turn without thinking is to stop our ears to this sane word from Jesus—a word that calls us to count the cost, to act with common sense.

II

Why is our Lord so insistent not only that we make a choice, but that we make that choice intelligently, that we make it in the light of the facts?

He is insistent upon this because he knows that to begin any enterprise without a thoughtful consideration of what we are undertaking and of the price to be paid is to court discouragement and disaster. While pastor in a certain city, I used to drive often by an imposing ruin. This ruin, I am told, had cost its builder almost a million dollars. It was a palace built of marble. But the man who had set out to build went broke before he could complete his task. So there stood this wreck with its glassless windows gazing out at the passers-by like the eyeless sockets of a skeleton. It was thus not a finished poem but only an ugly ruin, a monument to his failure to count the cost. All who passed by began to say that this man started to build and was not able to finish.

Many years ago a man came into the little village where we did our trading and proposed to build a railroad to connect us with another road that was some twenty-five miles away. Everybody greeted his proposal with enthusiasm. We were sure that this great tycoon was going to put us in touch with the outside world. Therefore, when he hired laborers and set them to throwing up a roadbed, we felt we were already in close contact with the great centers of our nation. But all our enthusiasm died a few days later when this tycoon ran out of money and left us with only an ugly heap of dirt less than a mile in length. That roadbed is there to this day, a monument not to the wisdom of this promising man, but to his stupidity. His decision was bold but not intelligent. Even courage to the point of recklessness is no substitute for good sense. It only leads to discouragement and disaster.

Had I been by when that scribe came to Jesus saying, "Master, I will follow thee whithersoever thou goest," I should have been thrilled. Not only so, but I should have expected a far greater thrill on the part of our Lord. But my expectations would have been disappointed. Instead of greeting this promising recruit with glad enthusiasm, he rather gave him this frosty answer:

"Foxes have holes, and birds of the air have nests; but the Son of man hath not where to lay his head."

Why did Jesus not meet his enthusiasm with a kindred enthusiasm? Why did he seem to repel him and to drive him away? It was not because he did not long for his loyalty even as he longs for yours and mine. It was because he saw that he was making his decision without regard to the facts. He knew that he was volunteering with his eyes shut and with his ears stopped. That Jesus was right is evidenced by the fact that when he disclosed to him that the master whom he was proposing to follow was more homeless than the foxes and more destitute than the birds of the air, he slipped away and we see his face no more. Jesus therefore calls for an intelligent decision because he knows that it is only as we choose intelligently that we are likely to see the enterprise through.

III

What, then, is involved in an intelligent choice?

First, if we are to build anything, we must face the fact that certain requirements are to be met by the builder. We can build nothing on our own terms. Whether we build a chicken coop or a cathedral, we must meet certain conditions. We can do nothing in this life unconditionally. Almost everybody would like a warm, rich, radiant religious experience if such could be had on our own terms. But whether we are building a henhouse or a skyscraper or a Christ-like character, there are certain conditions that must be met. These conditions are not optional, they are arbitrary.

Second, if we are to make an intelligent choice, not only must we realize that there are certain arbitrary conditions, but we must face the further fact that the greater the building, the greater must be our outlay. We do not expect to build a skyscraper at the same price we would expend upon a birdhouse. We do not expect a billion-dollar return on a one-dollar investment. We are to understand clearly that the greater our undertaking, the greater its cost. To ignore this is simply to court utter failure. This is what a certain psalmist meant when he said, "They that go down to the sea in ships, that do business in great waters; these see the works of the Lord and his wonders in the deep." He realized that it would be far safer for one to remain in his sleepy and quiet village. But he faced the further fact that by so remaining he would miss the thrill of seeing the "works of the Lord and his wonders in the deep." He knew that in order to see greatly we must adventure greatly.

The author of the book of Job was speaking to the same purpose when he asked a certain fisherman this quenching question: "Canst thou draw out leviathan with an hook?" Now, it is not certain whether leviathan is a crocodile or a whale. Assuming that the leviathan is a whale, this man was going out to catch the largest monster in the deep. We can approve of that. We love to see him as he hitches his wagon to a star. But our enthusiasm gives way to scornful laughter if we are hard of heart, or it gives way to tears of pity if we are tender of heart, when we see that he is trying to catch a whale with an ordinary hook. We know that he is doomed to disappointment, that he will in all probability come back a wet-blanket personality, cynically asserting that there is not a whale in the ocean, or if there is it cannot be caught.

IV

What does it cost to build?

Now since we can construct nothing on our own terms, it would be foolish to undertake the building of a Christlike character while ignoring the conditions. When the jailer asked of Paul, "What must I do to be saved?" that word "must" was surely the right word. There was something that he simply had to do if he was to find salvation. The conditions were and are absolutely arbitrary. We simply cannot be saved, on our own terms. God has no plan of salvation for an unsurrendered heart. Therefore if we are to build a Christlike character there is something that we must do.

Jesus never concealed this fact. He never disguised or softened the conditions. In speaking to this multitude he was frank to the point of seeming hard and repellent. Listen, "If any man come to me, and hate not his father, and mother, and wife, and children, and brethren, and sisters, yea, and his own life also, he cannot be my disciple." Of course, Jesus is not here using hate in the sense in which we use it. Nobody can be a Christian and hate anyone. Not only so, but being a Christian tones up and sweetens every human relationship. Every father is a better father for being a Christian, every wife a better wife for being a Christian. Nor are we to hate our lives. The best way to get ready for the life to come is to love this life and to live it as bravely and faithfully as we can.

What, then, does Jesus mean? He means this—that

he is to come first. He is to be so emphatically first that if there comes a time when a choice must be made between loyalty to him and loyalty to those who are nearest and dearest, then we must be loyal to him. He must be so emphatically first that we shall act in case of need as if our love for our dearest were no more than hate. If there comes a time when we must be loyal to him or lay down our lives, then we must not count our lives as dear unto ourselves. Our Lord must always come first. What, then, does it cost to build a Christlike character? It costs you, it costs all you have. Nothing less will do.

No more promising recruit ever came to Jesus than the rich young ruler. He seems to have had everything; cleanliness, enthusiasm, courage, love for the highest and best. In reverence he kneeled at the feet of Jesus, his eyes full of light and his face full of wistfulness to ask this question, "What must I do to inherit eternal life?" In reply Jesus gave a frank, full answer: "Go sell what you have, and give to the poor, and come, follow me." Then what? Here is the tragic answer: "He went away sorrowful."

Why did this promising young man miss the high quest upon which he had set out with such eagerness? One might say that he missed it because he would not sell what he had and give it to the poor. No, that was incidental. We must see through to what is fundamental in the story. The young man might have sold all he had and might have given every penny of it and still not have become a disciple. His failure was this—he refused to follow Jesus. However liberal and decent we may be, there is no building of a Christlike character without complete dedication of life. However faulty and frail we may be, if we give our all, then we can begin at once to build. How unpromising was that wreck who had wallowed in self-pity for thirty-eight years. He had no hope for himself. Nobody had any hope for him. When Jesus asked: "Do you want to get well?" his answer was a whine. Yet when even he willed what Jesus willed for him, the impossible became possible and he got upon his feet. Everybody can build who is willing to obey.

But there is another consideration that we must face if we are to reach a wise decision. That is this. If it costs to build, it also costs not to build. "If you lose your life," said Jesus, "you will find it. If you give it away, you will receive it back enriched." But if you seek to keep your life, you will lose it. I can imagine that I met this rich young ruler a few hours after his interview with Jesus. "The last time I saw you, you were at the feet of Jesus seeking eternal life. Did you find what you sought?"

"No," he answered, "I did not."

"Why?" I continued. "Was he not able to give life and give it in abundance?"

"I am sure he was quite able and willing," he replied. "The fact that I missed life was not his fault, but mine. I was not willing to pay the price. That was all—I was not willing to pay the price."

"What was the price?" I persisted.

"It was quite unreasonable," he answered. "It called for the giving up of everything in order to follow."

"Well," I replied, "I don't blame you in the least for refusing. It certainly seems a tremendous price to pay. I congratulate you on your wise choice. You can now go your own way keeping every penny that you possess."

But the young man did not share my enthusiasm. Instead we read of him, "He went away sorrowful." He might have gone with a song on his lips. But instead he went with a sob in his heart and with wretchedness looking out of his tired eyes. This was the case because in going away from Jesus he went away from life. Therefore every step that he took was a step toward death. It costs a great deal to build, there is no denying that. But it costs infinitely more not to build.

So the choice is for you and me today. It is said that years ago a great artist was spending a few days with some friends, and while there the little girl of the family received a silk fan as a birthday present. When she showed it to the artist, he said to her, "If you will let me keep this for a while, I'll paint you a picture on it."

But she snatched it away, saying, "You can't spoil my beautiful fan." But if she had left it in his hands, he would have given it back to her worth a thousandfold, and so Jesus comes asking for your life and mine. If we give them to him, he will give them back transfigured and transformed, for he is come that we might have life and that we might have it in abundance. What is your choice in the light of the facts as you see them in God's Word?

VI

FACING THE FACTS

"And when he came to himself, he said . . ."

LUKE 15:17

HERE IS A YOUNG MAN IN EARNEST CONVERSATION. He is not talking to a friend; he is talking to himself. We all talk to ourselves at times. Such conversations are important. They might be important because it is good to know what an intelligent person thinks. But they are important most of all because if you tell me what you habitually say to yourself, I will tell you what you are and what increasingly you are becoming. It is important to tell the truth at all times. "Speak every man truth with his neighbor," Paul urges, "for we are members one of another." Lying hurts the other fellow, but the most deadly form of lying is lying to oneself. To do that is to put a roadblock on your path to moral and spiritual progress.

Not only is this young man talking to himself, but he is telling himself the truth. You remember the woman with the shamefaced disease? She had suffered for twelve long years. She had gone to physician after physician who had relieved her of nothing but her money. Now that a new Physician has come, we hear her in conversation with herself. What is she saying? Had she told herself that she had recovered or that there was no chance of recovery even at the hands of Jesus, she would have hastened her steps toward the grave. But in spite of all her failures, what she said to herself was this: "If I can only touch his robe, I will recover." Thus encouraging herself, she found healing. This young man told himself the truth about himself. What was the arresting truth that as a fact-finding committee he brought out about himself?

I

And when he came to himself, he said, "I am in a mess." He faced the fact that he had thus far made a failure. He had spent a great deal. He had given up the privileges of home. He had given up fellowship with his father. He had spent all that he had. Having done this, what had he won? The best he could say for himself was this: "I perish with hunger. I have not found what I set out to find, I must confess, regardless of the purity or baseness of my motives. When I left home, I did not leave in order to disappoint my father. I did not leave in order to find the companionship of swine. I certainly did not leave in order to discover the pangs of hunger. But regardless of my motives, this is what has happened. Instead of finding satisfaction, I have found the anguish of starvation. I perish with hunger."

Now it strikes me that the confession made by this prodigal is largely characteristic of our generation. We are not greatly concerned about our wrongdoing. Our confessions of sin do not burst from us wet with tears and red with shame. But in spite of this we are keenly conscious of our emptiness. We are conscious of heart-hunger and of burning thirst. We are conscious, millions of us, of the fact that we have not found satisfaction for the deepest longings of our souls. Here is a minister congratulating one of the greatest actresses of the day. When he had finished reminding her of her vast achievements, she answered, "Don't talk to me about that. What I want is peace and rest, rest and peace." Well, that is what everybody wants, and that is what too few are finding.

When Jesus said to the woman at the well, "Whosoever drinketh of this water shall thirst again. But whosoever drinketh of the water that I shall give him shall never thirst" he was speaking home to a universal need. If we drink of the wells of this world, we do thirst again. What we all need is an inward well, a well that will make us independent of outward circumstances; one that when all outside resources are cut off can still supply our deepest needs. But vast numbers have missed that well. This is true not only of many outside the church but also of many that are within.

I have always had a profound sympathy for that fine churchman Nicodemus. He had given his life to the service of his faith. He was a clean, scholarly gentleman. But as he looked into his half-empty hands and into his half-empty heart, he said to himself, "I wonder if this is God's best for me." That wonder was brought to a climax when he heard that an exciting young rabbi was spending the night in Jerusalem. I imagine that it was only after a hard fight with himself that he made up his mind to go to see this rabbi. The fact that the friends of this churchman had turned their backs upon him and had denounced him naturally made him hesitate. Having decided to go, he went with fear and trembling. But in spite of his fears he did go. This he did because the hunger of his heart compelled him to go. Then when he came face to face with Jesus, our Lord spoke home to the longings of his soul rather than to the words of his lips by telling him how he could find life's fullest satisfaction.

"I perish with hunger." That is the conscious or unconscious declaration of millions. We affirm it by our mad pursuit of amusement. Winston Churchill said recently that England was standing upon a trap door, that at any moment she might plunge into an economic abyss. What was the matter? One big matter was this —she was spending her meager income on pleasures, amusements, gambling. In this country many are doing the same. It is our way of seeking a satisfaction that we have not found. Isaiah, if he were here now, would stand in front of these stampeding crowds as in the long ago and cry, "Wherefore do ye spend money for that which is not bread? and your labor for that which satisfieth not?" This prodigal honestly faced this fact: "I have made an adventure in quest of satisfaction, but it has been a keen disappointment. Instead of finding what I sought, I have found only a gnawing hunger."

II

When he came to himself, he said, "For the mess I am in I have nobody to blame but myself." Of course there are always those who may make it easier for us to go wrong and harder for us to go right. This seems to have been the case here. The friends of this prodigal do not show up well. They seem to have stood by only so long as their young friend had plenty. Therefore he might easily have blamed them. He might have found it easier still to blame his brother, that sun-tanned icicle who according to his own testimony had never committed a single sin in all his life. He might even have blamed his father. "Why," he might have snarled, "did he give me all that money and allow me to do as I pleased? He should have known that it would end like this."

Passing the blame, affirming "It is not my fault," is as common as it is deadly. It is as old as man. When Adam went wrong, Eve was to blame. But Eve was just as guiltless as Adam. The one really to blame was the serpent. This moral evasiveness is fatal. It ends by our putting the real blame upon God. All excuses for sin in reality condemn God. Omar Khayyam gives us an example of this:

> Oh, Thou, who Man of baser Earth didst make,
> And even with Paradise devise the Snake;
> For all the Sin wherewith the Face of Man
> —Is blackened Man's Forgiveness give—and take!

There you have it. But so long as we take this attitude, we never move one millionth of an inch towards God. This young man did dare, in spite of all his failure, to face this depressing fact—I have made a mess. I have done so by my own wrong choice. Therefore I have nobody to blame but myself.

FACING THE FACTS

III

And when he came to himself, he said, "Though I have missed the way and have missed it through my own fault, I do not have to keep on missing it. In spite of the fact that by my own choice I have left my father's house and have found only starvation, I can go back and find plenty. My father is the kindest of men. He will therefore treat me at least as well as he does his hired servants, and they have bread enough and to spare. Through my own wrong choice I am in a mess, but I do not have to remain as I am."

This is the very heart of the gospel. John tells us that Jesus gives us power to become. That is the most amazing power, it seems to me, in the universe. There is no measuring how greatly wrong we can go. But this is offset by the bracing fact that there is no measuring how greatly right we can go. From the very place on which I stand, two roads stretch away. One dips downward and ever downward until it loses itself in the quagmires of desolation and death; the other climbs upward and ever upward to where the light lingers even when the sun is set. I can take either road that I choose. Even so this young man, disappointed in himself, dared to say, "Though I am wrong, I can be right." That is what every sinner can say, however far from God he may have gone, however long he may have lingered in the far country.

IV

And when he came to himself, he said, "If I am to get out of this mess, if I am to get back home and into the fellowship of my father, the choice is up to me. If I do not desire to go back, no one in heaven or earth can compel me. If I do so desire, nobody on earth or in hell can prevent me. If I am ever to become what I ought to become, if I am ever to find satisfaction for the gnawing hungers and the burning thirsts of my soul, if I am ever to be able to be a channel of these satisfactions for others, I must do something about it. Nobody can do that but me; it is a choice that must be my very own."

Not only must I be willing to act, but I must be willing to do whatever is necessary in order to get back to my father's house. I came away by the road of self-will. In going back I must travel the one road that leads back into his fellowship, that is, the road of self-dedication. If you have decided to find good health, that means that you must be willing to obey the laws of health. This is the case because the road to health is not optional; it is arbitrary. If you have decided to win an education, you must take a certain road. That, too, is not optional but arbitrary. You cannot decide to know by simply rubbing a book on the top of your head once a month. If you have made up your mind to become a musician, narrow is the way. You must take the road that leads there. So if you have decided to go back to the peace and plenty of your Father's house, you must travel the one road that leads back, and that is the road of obedience, of self-surrender. The young man went away because he was determined to do as he pleased. His plea was "Give me." He can get back only by changing that "Give me" into "Make me." There is no road into the fellowship of God except the road of personal surrender.

Not only must he be willing to do something about it, not only must he be willing to do anything about it, but he must be willing to act in the here and now. He must bring his decision to the present moment, or it will come to naked nothing. This is true for all of us. We must act in the here and now because now is the only time we have. Yesterday has gone, tomorrow has not come—indeed it never will. The only time that our Lord offers us salvation is now. If we refuse to act in the now, if we refuse in the now to set our feet upon the road that leads back home, then we refuse forever.

Felix was deeply stirred by the preaching of Paul. We read that he shuddered. But he soothed his startled soul in this deadly fashion: "The preacher is telling the truth. I am deeply concerned about what he says. I am so deply concerned that one day I am going to take him seriously. In some tomorrow when there is a convenient season, I am going to make my high decision." But what he really said was this: "In spite of the fact that I see clearly the choice that I ought to make, regardless of the cost to myself or to others, I am not going to make the decision now. Thus refusing to choose the way of Christ in the here and now, he refused forever. There is but one way back to God, and that is to turn to him in the here and now.

V

When this young man thus faced the facts about himself, that he was wrong, that he could be right, and when he put his knowledge into action, what happened?

IN PARABLES

Here is the thrilling answer: "But when he was yet a great way off, his father saw him, and had compassion and ran, and fell on his neck and kissed him." In his compassion the father shared his heartache, felt the gnawing of his hunger, blushed in his shame. Then he commanded, "Bring quickly the best robe and put it on him, and put a ring on his hand and shoes on his feet; and bring the fatted calf and kill it; and let us eat and be merry." The whole story has in it an atmosphere of hot haste, of enthusiastic eagerness. But you will notice that all the haste is on the part of the father; none on the part of the son. It is Jesus' way of telling us that God is in an all but infinite hurry to give heaven's best to us; that he will do this the very moment that we by our turning make such giving possible.

I bring you, therefore, this question: If you have not found satisfaction for the deepest hungers of your heart, who is to blame? Who is responsible for the delay? It is not God, but you. Often I have heard the story of wrestling Jacob referred to as an ideal picture of conversion. It is certainly a beautiful and thrilling story. It is almost unbelievable that this man who had been a trickster so long that he had become convinced that a crooked line was the shortest distance between two points could ever be remade. Yet even Jacob was reborn. There is something vastly gripping in seeing him as he limps away in the light of the morning with the beams of the Son of Righteousness shining on his face and in his heart. He has been given a new name to match his new nature.

But we need to remember that the blessing which came to Jacob in the light of the early morning might

70

have come much sooner. It might have been his in the twilight of the previous evening. In fact, it might have been his years before. Who had held it up? Not God, but Jacob. "There wrestled with him a man," says the story. Why was there any wrestling at all? It was because Jacob resisted God. Where there is no resistance, there can be no wrestling. I remember a schoolmate of my boyhood days. Though wrestling was at that time very popular, he would flatly refuse to participate. Often we tried to force him, but our efforts were in vain. This was the case because when we laid violent hands on him, he would crumple up in a heap like a sack of sand. Nobody could compel him to wrestle because he surrendered without it. The only reason for the all-night wrestling was Jacob's stubborn resistance of God. The very moment that he ceased to wrestle and came to yield, that moment God gave him a new nature and a new name. Even so he will do for us the moment we yield. This is the promise: "Behold, now is the accepted time; behold, now is the day of salvation."

VII

SOUR SAINTS

"Thou never gavest me a kid, that I might make merry with my friends."

LUKE 15:29

W HAT AN UGLY TEXT! IT IS A CROSS BETWEEN A snarl and a whine. Yet this is the testimony of a very earnest and upright man who has spent every day of his life in his father's house. According to his own testimony he has been a most dutiful son. Indeed, he has been perfect. Never once has he transgressed his father's commandments. Yet all his uprightness and industry have brought him naked nothing. "Thou never gavest me a kid," he tells his father, and sad to say, his father does not and cannot deny the charge.

This chap represents that ugly company of the soured saints. He is one of those unfortunate creatures whose religion has been sheer drudgery. Of course, it was his own fault. The father was infinitely eager to share his very all with him. "Son, thou art ever with me, and all that I have is thine." But in spite of the father's eagerness, the son

72

was as completely famished as his prodigal brother in the far country.

Naturally we do not admire this elder son. Were we in search of the life abundant, we should never think of asking him the way to find it. Were we tortured by more heartache than we knew how to handle in our own strength, we should never think of turning to him. Even Jesus, who had such a keen eye for the best in us, has nothing good to say about him. But we are not to conclude from that that this elder son was utterly bad. He was not. No man is. In spite of the fact that he is so disappointing, he still had something to say for himself.

I

What can we say in his favor?

1. Since he represents the typical Pharisee, we can be sure that he was an honest and upright man, utterly free from the ugly sins of the flesh. His story opens with an assertion that he was in the field; that is, he was in a clean environment. He was out where the blue skies bent about his head, where the fresh winds brought to him the aroma of the upturned sod or the sweet fragrance of new-mown hay. He was in a clean environment. He was in this clean environment of his own choice. He was there because he desired to be there.

But where was his brother? He was in a pigsty. He was in a foul and filthy environment. He was there because of his own choice. His were the sins of the flesh. He had wasted his substance with riotous living. Therefore, we must conclude that this elder son was in this respect leagues ahead of his younger brother. One was clean, and the other unclean. Neither God nor man can set a premium on profligacy.

2. The fact that this elder son was in the field indicates that he was a worker. Work is every man's obligation. Bernard Shaw said that a gentleman is a man who puts into life more than he takes out. This sour saint was on the way to being a gentleman. Work is a roadway to self-respect. Work is godlike. Jesus said, "My Father worketh hitherto, and I work." He seems to add this last word with a holy swagger. He was glad to be one of the world's workers. But while this son was working, his younger brother was wasting. Here again he was leagues ahead of him.

3. Being a clean and earnest worker, he was making a contribution. So far as the prodigal was concerned, the farm might be turned back to the wilderness. So far as he seemed to care, the whole place might topple into ruins. But the elder son kept the farm going. He helped to keep the home place capable of receiving his prodigal brother when his debauch was over.

In another story of Jesus, the parable of the Pharisee and the publican, our sympathies are all with the publican, in spite of the fact that we know he was a renegade and a traitor to his country. We watch the Pharisee with huge disapproval as he stalks his way into the temple and utters his proud prayer with a good eye on himself, a bad eye on his brother, and no eye on the Lord at all. But in spite of all his faults we need to bear in mind that it was his loyalty to his religion that had built the temple and kept it open. But for him, with all his ugliness, there would have been no place of prayer to which this publican could have turned when his black hour of need was upon him. This elder son, therefore, has something to say for himself.

II

But in spite of all this decency and industry he is vastly disappointing. He is disappointing to his father and to his brother and to himself. He is disappointing to us. What is the matter with him?

1. Fundamentally he had one central defect. Though he was a member of a family, he was totally lacking in the family spirit of love and loyalty and good will. His whole story indicates that he was on good terms neither with his father nor with his brother. Though bound up in a bundle of life with others, he insisted on thinking and acting as if he were a lone wolf.

It was this lack of the family spirit that was back of all that was ugly and ruinous in his life. It is this lack of family spirit that accounts for the major tragedies of human history. How to live together has been a problem ever since Cain killed Abel. It has become more intense as all the nations have come to experience the proximity of the family without the family spirit. This lack spells tragedy both to the group and to the individual.

Look how it worked for this elder son. One day tragedy struck. The heavy news came that his gay and attractive younger brother had headed for the far country. That news broke his father's heart. He could not shut his eyes to the lines of suffering in that kindly face. But he himself had no fellowship in his suffering. He shrugged it off. He declared that it was none of his business, that he was broad-minded, that he believed in letting every man go to hell in his own way. So if this young fool wanted to squander his treasure in that fashion, let him do so. It was not his lookout.

Now, failing to care that his brother was wasting his substance in riotous living, he failed to do anything about it. He failed even to try. He was interested in keeping up the institution of the farm, but he was indifferent as to the individual. Even had he sought to help with his loveless hands, I do not think that he would have accomplished much. A saintly prisoner whose task was nursing declared that the skills of the nursing profession are altogether secondary. He declared further that if he had his way, he would allow no loveless nurse to approach a suffering patient; that such a nurse would only scatter poison instead of bringing healing.

It strikes me that there is no more dangerous, no more cruel sin than that of indifference, the ability to look upon the woes and wounds of others and be totally unmoved. When I think of the most hellish single sentence that I ever read, I think of one that we read in the Gospels. Judas has just betrayed his Lord. After he committed that sin, remorse laid its torturing hands upon him and thrusts him into hell. In his agony he feels that he must find relief.

Where does he turn in his hour of desperation? He does not turn to Jesus, whom he has betrayed. That was his most ruinous sin. The greatest wrong Judas did to Jesus was not in betraying with his kiss, but in his failure to come back after his ghastly sin and permit his Lord to forgive him. How that would have gladdened Jesus! It would also have made Judas one of the beautiful saints of sacred history.

But though he refused to come back to the Master

whom he had betrayed, he did not repudiate religion altogether. He turned to the priests, the ministers of his church, the kind of men who had taught him in childhood. These men could have helped him. However crimson his guilt, they had a word in their own scriptures that said, "Though your sins be as scarlet, they shall be as white as snow." But they did not give this broken man that assurance. Instead, they answered his confession of guilt with this most devilish of all words, "What is that to us? See thou to that."

I wonder how many of us have made that statement, if not with our lips, then with our lives? It is so easy not to care. I had a friend in college who had deep scars upon his soul because of the kind of home into which he was born. Outwardly gay, he was inwardly tortured. Once as we talked far into the night, he said this pathetic word: "For ten years I have gone to bed with the secret wish that I might not wake in the morning."

One Sunday I went with this young man to hear a minister who at that time was one of the best known ministers in America. He preached a brilliant and scholarly sermon, but as we came away I asked my friend, "How did you like him?" With considerable bitterness he answered, "He reminded me of a man standing at a safe distance on the shore watching some poor chap drown, and saying, 'You fool, you. You ought to be able to swim like I can.'" No criticism could be more devastating than that. I am not going to throw a stone at this minister. I might wound myself.

2. A second ugliness on the part of this elder son grew naturally out of the first. Failing to care that his brother had gone away, he had no joy in his return. The father

was glad beyond all words. The home atmosphere was vibrant with happiness. Even the hired servants had a share in it, but not this elder son. Refusing to share the family obligations and responsibilities, he was incapable of sharing the family's privileges and joys. While laughter lightened all other faces, his remained dark.

Not only did he fail to share in the joy at his brother's homecoming, but that coming made him positively angry. He felt that he had a right to be angry. He was quite sure that his was righteous indignation. That is the kind of indignation that we in the church generally claim, but too often our claims are false, sad to say. The truth is that righteous indignation is a rather rare commodity. It is also as priceless as it is rare. There are few things that we need more today than righteous indignation. To be wanting in it is a sad defect. It indicates that we have become morally flabby, if not positively rotten.

But was this elder brother righteously indignant? I think not. Righteous indignation has at least two characteristics. First, it is born of love, and not of selfishness and hate. When certain adults sought to prevent little children crowding into the arms of Jesus, our Lord became indignant. His indignation was born of his love for children. One day when he went into a synagogue and saw a man with a withered hand, he was eager to heal him. But when he sought to work this miracle over the protest of certain petty religionists who thought more of their own regulations than of giving this unfortunate man a chance, Mark tells us that Jesus looked upon them with anger. His anger was born

SOUR SAINTS

of his love both for the needy man and for those wicked men who were seeking to rob him of his chance.

But while Jesus blazed with anger when he saw right trodden under foot of might, when he saw weakness crushed by strength, he never resented an affront to himself. He was slandered as few men have ever been slandered. There were those who declared that he was a glutton and a drunkard. There were those who claimed that he did his works of wonder in the power of demons rather than the power of God. Once he had his face slapped. But at none of these did he blaze with anger. I think that fact impressed tempestuous Simon as much as anything that Jesus ever did. Forty years later he wrote, "When he was reviled, he reviled not again."

A second characteristic of righteous anger is that it seeks to help and not to hurt. When Jesus grew angry, he rebuked those who angered him for their own good. Not only so, but he suffered for them. He never sought to hurt, but always to help.

Now, neither of these characteristics belonged to the anger of this elder son. His anger was born not of his love, but of his envy. It was a child of hate. Not only was it the child of hate, but it sought to hurt rather than to help. He refused to go into the feast, not to help his faher but to spite him. He refused to go into the feast because he was determined to put this profligate brother in his place.

His, therefore, was the type of anger that is so common and so hurtful among us. Drummond was of the opinion that this type of selfish anger causes more grief and more tears than almost anything else in the world. This is the case because when we are angered we seek to wound the one who angers us. Even certain psychologists seem to encourage such a procedure. They seem to think that if husband and wife get a bit angry, it relieves the situation for them to unsheath the sword of their tongue and stab right and left. Even Tennyson sings,

Blessing on the falling out that all the more endears,
When we fall out with those we love and kiss again with
    tears.

Well, I seriously question whether any falling out really endears, and as for kissing again with tears, I prefer my kisses with another kind of sauce.

So hurtful is anger that we doubt the vital Christianity of those who constantly give way to it. A minister of my acquaintance said that while pastor of a small village church there was one woman in his congregation who was an outstanding leader. Her husband, a good and upright man and the leading merchant of the village, while friendly to religion, was not a member of the church. This merchant and the minister were close friends. Naturally the minister sought earnestly to win him, but failed. One day he said to him, "John, I have done everything I know how to do. You still stand out. I think at least you ought to tell me why you do not accept Jesus Christ and come into the church with your wife and children."

Then with great reluctance the merchant replied, "Perhaps you have a right to know. I will tell you. In so doing I hope you do not think I am reflecting upon my wife. She is the best woman in your church. You could not run your church without her. Still she has this one big fault, a vicious temper. Now and then she goes into a tantrum. When she does, the children and I have to take to the woods. It is hard for me to believe in that type of Christianity."

The preacher was a brave man. In proof of that he went at once to the wife and told her what her husband had said. He looked for her to blaze, but instead her eyes filled with tears as she said, "He is exactly right. I have been ashamed and grieved over my temper many times, but what am I to do about it?" Then the minister told her that the fruit of the Spirit is love, joy, peace, long-suffering, gentleness, goodness, meekness, faithfulness, self-control. Then they knelt in prayer together, inviting the Spirit of self-control to come into her heart.

A few days later this merchant was preparing to go fishing. He walked into the living room with a long bamboo rod upon his shoulder. It so happened that they had just hung a beautiful lamp in that living room. It looked as if it had come out of Arabian nights. But it was defectively hung. Therefore, when this husband turned about with his bamboo rod over his shoulder, he sideswiped that lamp and it came crashing down, sounding like a hardware store washing away in a thunderstorm. He stood there shaking in his shoes waiting for the storm of temper. When it didn't come, he thought his wife must be absent. But a moment later he discovered her smiling at him over the banister. He joined the church next Sunday.

I wish I might report such a victory for this elder son, but I cannot. He was too good to associate with his prodigal brother; therefore he was incapable of association with his father. Refusing that association with both son and father, he missed the feast. He shut the door in his own face. He tore up his ticket. There is only one ticket of admission into this feast. It has upon it this inscription, "By this shall all men know that ye are my disciples, if ye have love one to another." Without that ticket not even God can get you into the feast. With that ticket the door will open of its own accord.

VIII

PERSONAL PREACHING

"And when the chief priests and the Pharisees had heard his parables, they perceived that he spake of them."

MATTHEW 21:45

THAT WAS PERSONAL PREACHING. THAT IS THE ONLY kind of preaching that is of real value. By this I do not mean that the minister is to deal in personalities. He is not to make of his pulpit an ambush behind which to hide while he cannonades those who may have persecuted or spitefully used him. To use the pulpit in that fashion is as wicked and witless as it is cowardly. Jesus was never guilty of such a foolish and evil practice. He never preached in order to get back at his enemies. But while refusing thus to take vengeance on his foes, he did make every hearer feel that he was speaking to him personally.

To get such response from these chief priests and Pharisees required real skill. Of course, there is a skill in missing as there is in hitting. A friend told me some time ago of watching an expert dagger thrower. This man stood a woman dressed in tights against a dark wall.

He then drew an exact profile of her body with these sharp daggers. Every dagger that he threw came very close, but not one touched. He never drew a drop of blood. He missed as completely as the minister who preaches to those who are absent or to the man in the moon.

It required skill to strike home to these hearers because they were such artful dodgers. Years ago I attended a state fair. Here I saw a booth where for a nominal sum anyone so inclined might throw baseballs at a man whose head was projecting through a hole in a thick canvas only a few yards away. There were those kindly enough to try their skill. But while I watched there was not a single hit. However skillful those worthy men may have been at throwing, the man thus exposing himself was even more skillful in dodging. Yet I dare say that even he was a mere amateur as an artful dodger in comparison with these chief priests and Pharisees. But in spite of all their skill it stands written in the record: "They perceived that he spake of them."

I

"And when the chief priests and the Pharisees heard his parables. . . ."

These parables that they heard are the two that immediately follow. They have an interesting background.

These church officials have come to Jesus with a legitimate question. "By what authority," they asked, "are you doing these things?" What things? Well, Jesus was doing quite a lot. He had cleansed the temple, seeking to make it once more into a house of prayer rather than a place of buying and selling. He was healing the sick, preaching amazing sermons, upsetting things generally. With wisdom, therefore, they asked by what authority.

In reply Jesus said, "I will answer your question provided you will answer one for me. The baptism of John —was it from heaven or of men?" By baptism Jesus means the whole ministry of John. This was the question: Was John a prohpet, or was he an imposter? At that, the record says, they argued among themselves. Their argument was not as how best to get at the truth, but as to what lie would be most plausible and profitable. A keen young lawyer told me that he often said to his witnesses, "Don't tell that lie; tell this one." Thus arguing, they concluded: "If we say John was a real prophet, that will embarrass us, for he will then ask why we did not believe him. If we say that he was an imposter, then we shall arouse the indignation of the multitude, for they count John as a prophet." Therefore they decided to be neutral. Not knowing what church to join, they did not join any. Thus they answered, "We do not know." In reply Jesus said, "Neither will I tell you by what authority I do these things."

Why did our Lord give such an answer? It was not because of anger or because he was seeking to get back at his foes. He knew that a factual answer would be useless. He knew that there was no use in broadcasting to a group that had put its receiving set out of commission. They simply did not desire to know the truth. Jesus spoke and still speaks to everybody who is willing to hear. When he first met Pilate, he answered him eagerly and earnestly. He told him that he was a king in the realm of the truth. He even opened the door of that kingdom to him and invited him to enter. But when

Pilate became a creature of shifts and devices, when he smashed his receiving set by refusing to hear, Jesus spoke to him no more.

In all Jerusalem there was perhaps not a man more eager to meet Jesus than was Herod. He desired to see him do some sleight of hand trick, some work of wonder. But Jesus disappointed him. Not once did he speak to this foxy man. Why? Not because he was angry at the renegade. He refused because he knew that to speak would do no good. Not too long ago Herod had listened to John the Baptist. Not only so, but he had been deeply stirred. I can imagine that he even looked wistfully toward the heights and longed to climb. But in spite of that fact he never did. Thus shutting his eyes, he descended to such depths that he at last served the prophet's head to his mistress as he might have served a platter of roast pig. Thus he had blinded his eyes and stopped his ears. There are some even now to whom Jesus will not speak, for if he should, it would do no good because they refuse to hear.

II

Now, since these religious leaders had taken a position of neutrailty, Jesus saw that he could not enter their hearts by a direct road. Therefore he sought to enter by a road that was indirect. To that end he told them two stories. By showing them other offenders, he compelled them to see themselves. By leading them to sit in judgment upon these, he compelled them to bring in a verdict against themselves.

Look at the first of these stories: A certain father had two sons. This father said to the first son, "Go work

today in my vineyard." The son replied in a thoroughly
churlish fashion. His answer was a brutal "I will not."
He was not even decently polite. He represented the
publicans and harlots of the day. These had broken
with the church. They were rank outsiders. Knowing
not the law they were under a curse. For them the
church of that day had no care and felt no responsi-
bility.

To the second son the father gave the same command.
But how different was his response! This son gave exactly the answer that any father would be glad to hear.
With genuine courtesy he said, "I go, sir." But though
he promised to go, he did not. He thought that a pledge
to obey was the same as obeying. He thought that to
unite with the church and to assume its vows was enough.
Having taken this right action, he could then sit down
and do nothing. Therefore, having promised to go, he
refused to go. Whereas the churlish son, in spite of his
brutal refusal, having thought the situation over, decided to obey.

Then Jesus pressed home the question; "Which of
these sons did the will of his father?" "The one who
obeyed," came the right and ready answer. "That,"
replied Jesus, "is exactly what the harlots and sinners
did when they heard the preaching of John the Baptist.
That is what you refused to do. Not only did you refuse
to respond to his preaching, but you refused to be moved
by the results of that preaching. John's preaching re-
sulted in changed lives. These outcasts for whom you
had neither hope nor care were remade. But that fact
made no impression upon you. You refused to believe
both the message and the results, both the preaching

and the works. Since you did not go to work in the vineyard, according to your own verdict you are guilty of disobedience. You have not done the will of your Father.

III

"Not only," continued Jesus, "have you refused to work in the vineyard, but you have been guilty of positive rebellion." Then he told this second story of the householder who planted a vineyard, rented it out to tenants, and went into a far country. That was something that happened often in those days. It is something that has been done through the centuries. Almost every farmer knows what it is to rent land for a share of the crop. Every tenant expects to pay either in money or in the fruits of the field.

But when the householder sent to his tenants for his share of the fruit, they refused to give it. Not only so, but "they took his servants and beat one, killed another, and stoned another." But the lord of this vineyard was a patient man. Therefore he sent other servants, more than the first, but with the same tragic results. At last he sent his son, saying, "They will respect my son." But they were even more eager to kill him than they had been to kill the servants. This was the case because they were sure that if they got him out of the way, the inheritance would be theirs.

In the language of the farmer Jesus was here "plowing very close to the corn." These religious leaders to whom he was speaking had already taken over the inheritance. They were sure that the church of that day was their very own. They had grown fat upon its revenues. They had become autocratic in wielding its power. There is no doubt that it was the threat of Jesus to the prestige and power of these usurpers that kindled in them a hot anger that could not be satisfied by anything short of his death on the cross.

Nor is this the only time that such a tragic situation has developed. There have always been those who were eager to push God out and take over for themselves. I have known more than one church dignitary who impressed me as conscientiously believing that his was the final authority in the church. Such a man is always a bit of a pest because nobody is quite so hopelessly wrong as the man who is conscientiously wrong. I have met one or two pastors who seemed to me to feel that the church ought to minister to them rather than they to the church. At rare intervals I have even known an ambitious layman who appeared to be convinced that he had a perfect right to dominate his local church; that both pastor and people were but "pieces of the game he plays." It is quite human to desire to be "lords over God's heritage." It is also quite wicked.

Now, having told his story, Jesus pressed home this question: What will the owner of the vineyard do to these servants? The chief priests and Pharisees gave a prompt answer. "He will put the wretches to a miserable death, and let out the vineyard to other tenants who will give him the fruits in their season." Thus Jesus compelled them to face the facts about themselves. But though they had pronounced themselves guilty, they did not change. They flatly refused to repent. Instead of taking sides against their sin, they took sides against the Saviour. Instead of hating the disease, they hated and crucified the Physician. Thus their story had a tragic ending. The Kingdom was taken from them. Because of their refusal to repent some died physically; all died spiritually. But it need not have been the case. Their story might have ended in triumph.

IV

Here is another story that has much in common, yet it ended not in defeat but in victory. David in hot blood has become guilty of adultery. In cold blood he has committed murder. Not only so but instead of facing his ghastly guilt, he seeks to rationalize, to plead not guilty. Having ordered that his faithful and loyal servant Uriah be put at the forefront of the attack, then abandoned, he had murdered him as ruthlessly as if he had stabbed him in the back. Yet when a messenger came telling the king that his plan for murder had been put through with success, he remarked piously, "the sword devoureth one as well as another." Here is a new low in sheer heartless hypocrisy. In all the Bible there is not a more hideous crime than that of this shepherd king.

But one day his faithful minister, the prophet Nathan, dared to make David a pastoral call. It was not an easy thing to do. Having obtained an audience, after the manner of Jesus, he told the king a story. It was the story of a poor man who possessed no flocks and herds but only one lamb. That lamb was especially dear to him. It was prized not simply for its intrinsic value, but as a pet. It had become like a member of the family. But when a wealthy neighbor whose flocks and herds were numbered by the hundreds had a guest, he

90

refused to take a lamb of his own though it would not have been missed. Instead he cruelly stole and slaughtered the one lamb of his poor neighbor.

When David heard that story of rank injustice, his cheeks fairly flamed with anger, and his eyes flashed fire. Sin looks so much more ugly in our neighbor than it does in ourselves. Then in the name of justice he passed sentence upon the offender. "Guilty," he said. "The man that did that shall die." At that Nathan got personal. I heard a minister say that the prophet shook his finger in David's face and shouted in thunder tones, "Thou art the man." Well, he has as much right to his opinion as I do to mine. But I do not think it happened that way at all. Instead, I am inclined to believe that Nathan with great tenderness and yearning said, "Thou art the man." I think he spoke to his king as if he were just dying to see him repent. Judging by the results I am convinced that every single syllable came from a broken and bleeding heart, baptized in tears.

Then what? It would have been so easy for this proud king to have grown angry as did the chief priests and Pharisees. He might have had the prophet flung into prison or executed. But instead of thus taking sides against the preacher, he took sides against his sin. Instead of getting angry at the physician, he turned in hatred upon his disease. Therefore his knees went weak, and he clutched at God's skirts and cried, "Have mercy upon me." Nor did he cry in vain, for God always waits to forgive and to forget. Thus this murderer became one of the saints of sacred story.

This gospel of ours is a gospel for sinners, and for sinners only. Here is a word that fits us all: "There is no difference, for all have sinned and come short of the glory of God." This means you. This means me. We can refuse to repent, as did these religious leaders, and lay hold on death. We can repent as did David and find life. Thus "I have set before you life and death, blessing and cursing: therefore choose life." Who is to make that choice? "Thou art the man."

IX

CHOKED LIVES

"And some fell among thorns, and the thorns grew up, and choked it, and it yielded no fruit."

MARK 4:7

T HIS IS PART OF THE PARABLE OF THE SOWER. IT IS a story of failure. It is a failure all the more tragic because there were such fine possibilities of victory. Here and there along the way I have been thrilled by those who, having very little, have made so much out of that little. Take the woman at the well for instance. I should never have chosen her as a promising evangelist. Not that she had not once possessed charm, she had. Any woman who could marry five times has some charm. But she is tarnished now, and has large ly given herself up. Thus she has come to the well at the noon hour today, not to meet Jesus, but because she is less afraid of the hot sun than she is of the hot scorn of her decent sisters who visit the well only in the cool of the day.

But after this interview with our Lord I see her as, forgetful of her errand, she leaves her water vessel and starts back to the village. When I remind her of her forgetfulness, she refuses to listen. Then I say, "Why the hurry?" "I am going to tell the villagers about Jesus," she replies. At that I laugh out loud and say in bitter scorn, "You? Why, you have been blown like a dirty rag about the streets of this village for years. After the way you have lived, you are going to tell about Jesus?" But in spite of me she goes on her mission. Therefore it stands written in the record, "Many . . . believed on him for the saying of the woman."

Now, you and I have had a far better opportunity than she. This man of our story had a far better opportunity, yet how much did he do with it? How much have we done with our opportuinties? How many have believed because of what we are and of what we have said? This man as some of us made a failure. It was a failure, I repeat, that was all the more tragic because his story might have been so beautifully different.

I

Look at the opportunities that were his.

1. He was a man of gifts. This is indicated by the fact that he could grow such a luxurious crop of thorns. Any soil that can grow luxurious thorns can also grow luxurious grain. The fact that a man can go greatly wrong is an indication that he can go greatly right. Our power to become is the most amazing fact about us. It is beyond belief how vastly right we can go and how vastly wrong we can go. This man had a great capacity for becoming something wonderful and worthful.

2. Second, he had heard the word. He had exposed himself to that gospel which is the power of God unto

salvation. That also is true of you and me. From our very childhood we have known the Holy Scriptures that are able to make us wise unto salvation through faith that is in Christ Jesus. This gospel has been our priceless possession from youth's bright morning. It may have become a bit commonplace to us. To some, maybe, familiarity has bred a measure of contempt. But if we have eyes to see and ears to hear, it is still our most priceless possession. This man had heard the gospel.

3. Not only had he heard the gospel, but he had heard it responsively. That is indicated by his story. Now, it is possible to hear this amazing gospel and be moved by it and yet not be moved enough. Felix was greatly stirred at the preaching of Paul, so greatly stirred that he felt sure he would be a Christian sometime, in fact almost any time except the present. But he said, "Go thy way for this time." Herod was greatly moved by the preaching of John the Baptist. The story says that he did many things. But he failed to do the main thing; he failed to yield himself to God.

This man not only had heard but had responded. His story, I can imagine, would read a bit like that of Matthew. "And as Jesus passed forth from thence, he saw a man, named Mathew, sitting at the receipt of custom: and he saith unto him, 'follow me.' " What then? Did Matthew sob? I do not know. Did he sing? I do not know. Did he shout? I do not know. I only know that he did the essential thing. He rose up and followed him. The man of this story once heard the gospel message, and having heard it, he said, "I will arise and go to my father." Therefore he is a man from whom we have the right to expect rich and abundant fruit. Yet he became utterly useless.

II

What was it that wrecked him?

It was not the fact that having made a decision to follow Christ one day, the very next he decided against it. He was not like those who in the long ago heard Jesus preach a sermon that shocked them, that amazed and offended them. Their story reads like this: "Many of the disciples went back, and walked no more with him." This man did not make a clean break with Jesus. He did not make a clean break with his church. In all probability he remained in the church to the very end of his days.

No more did this man fail out of sheer laziness. He did not fail because he put his personal comfort above character. Many do fail after that fashion. That is one cause of the failure of the man of one talent. His lord called him slothful. That is the secret of the failure of another man whose garden was full of thorns. "I went by the field of the slothful, . . . and, lo, it was all grown over with thorns." But those thorns were there, not because the sluggard in energetic anger had planted them. The thorns were there because he had neglected his garden. Whenever we neglect our garden, by that very neglect we turn it back to the wilderness.

Why, I repeat, did this man fail? It was not because he was lazy and idle and sluggish. It was not because he was not busy. It was rather because he was too busy. It was not for lack of purpose. It was because of too many purposes. He got so interested in the secondary that he forgot the primary. He is a bit like that chap in that Old Testament parable. You remember he was given a prisoner to guard. The guarding of that prisoner was so important that he was told he would have to give up his own life if he should permit him to escape. But in spite of that solemn warning he did permit him to escape. When he was called on the carpet, he could not say, "I did my best but was overpowered." All he could say was, "and as thy servant was busy here and there, he was gone." He had allowed the essential to be crowded out by the nonessential.

III

What are some of the thorns that crowd the grain out of our lives?

Of course, the grain may be crowded out by positive wrongdoing. We all realize that fact. Since that is so evident, it is not one of the thorns against which we are warned by our Lord. But whether we are positive wrongdoers or not, the danger of allowing some kind of thorn to mar our usefulness is one that is ever with us.

Paul faced it in his own life. He was a man who had been wonderfully converted. He was a man who had enjoyed a growing fellowship with Jesus Christ. He had passed on from the "these things" of his conversion to the "those things" of a richer spiritual experience. He had been mightily used. Few men have ever surpassed him in that. It would be almost impossible to exaggerate the usefulness of this great man. Yet he faced the fact that even he might become useless. Therefore he said, "I keep under my body, and bring it into subjection:

lest that by any means, when I have preached to others, I myself should be a castaway."

Jesus mentions three kinds of thorns that often crowd the wheat out of our lives.

1. The cares of this world. In other words, worry. Jesus was a determined foe of worry. Three times over in the sixth chapter of the Gospel of Matthew he warns us against it. He knows that worry may cheat the one who worries, and by cheating the one who worries it may cheat others. The man who is constantly worried cannot possibly be as fruitful as he would if he had peace in his heart. Worry is a white-collar sin that threatens the religious oftentimes quite as much as it does those who make no pretention to religion.

Had you inquired in Bethany nineteen hundred years ago for the best woman of the village, you would have found yourself a few moments later knocking on the door of Martha. Here was the home that Jesus loved the best. I dare say that he felt far more at home here than he did in the one at Nazareth. Yet one day when he came unexpectedly, his day was largely spoiled, as well as that of Mary, and Martha's day was worse than spoiled. This was the case not because this favorite guest was not welcome; it was spoiled because Martha got so worried over the dinner that she was unable to enjoy what would otherwise have been one of the loveliest days of her life. Worry is a thorn that often crowds out the wheat both of joy and of usefulness.

2. A second type of thorn that Jesus mentions is delight in riches. Here, as so often, Jesus is warning us about money. Money is not bad in itself, but to delight in riches is to love riches. "How hard it is," said Jesus

after the failure of the young ruler, "for them that trust in riches to enter into the kingdom." Yes, and how hard it is for them that have riches to remain active and enthusiastic in the kingdom.

I have driven in the lovely surburbs of my city, past the gracious homes of some of my people, and my heart has gone out in sympathy toward them. They were well-wishers. They were right-thinking people. They were as decent as decency. But I knew that in any hard-fought campaign I could not as a rule count on them. They were so mired in a thousand social and business engagements that they had no time for tasks of supreme importance.

Money can be very possessive. I saw two flies walking beside a ten-acre field this past summer. At least it looked like a ten-acre field to them; it was a piece of Tanglefoot. The younger fly said to the older, "What do you think of this stuff called Tanglefoot?"

"I am opposed to it," the older said.

"What is the matter?" came the reply. "Is it poisonous?"

"Not a bit of it."

"Is it bitter?"

"No, it is rather sweet."

"Then, what are your objections?"

About that time a friend of theirs settled down in the middle of that flypaper. "My flypaper," he said proudly. But the flypaper said, "My fly." Then his friend remarked sadly, "You will never see him in church anymore. He possesses wealth, but he is more possessed by his wealth."

A few years ago I went to hold a meeting in a church

where I had formerly been pastor. Among the old friends I met there was a former neighbor, a member of another denomination. He was, I think, during my pastorate the most useful man in his church and one of the most useful and influential in his city. In the course of our conversation he said, "I have made more money this year than I have made in all of the rest of my life together."

"Good," I replied. "That is fine if you can manage it."

"Yes," he replied, "I entered the oil game and I struck it rich."

But I felt that there was something wanting. Therefore I asked him a question, "How is your church getting on?"

The enthusiasm died in his voice. "You know," he replied, "I am not attending church with the regularity I once did. I got so absorbed in the oil game."

"How," I continued, "is that fine Sunday-school class? You used to teach a class of seventy teen-age boys, and you grappled them to you with hoops of steel. How is your class getting on?"

His enthusiasm then died to utter nothingness as he answered, "I have had to give up my class. I got so busy in the oil business."

He was not a bad man. He was a man who had let the delight in being rich crowd out the grain of a useful life.

3. A third type of thorn that Jesus mentions covers a wide field, "the desire for other things." That is, said Jesus, "Anything is a thorn, however good or bad, that

crowds out the wheat." For instance, I think it is quite right for me as a pastor to wish to be popular with my people, to desire the approval of the congregation which I am called to serve. That is not a matter of mere vanity. It is essential to my highest usefulness. I do not care how true may be the message that I bring, if you resent me, if you feel hard against me, I can do little for you. It is almost essential that I in some measure win you to myself as a first step to winning you to my Lord.

Yet, while it is very good to be popular and to have the approval of my congregation, if I put that first, then it becomes a deadly danger and a thorn. I read of certain people in John's Gospel who were greatly impressed by Jesus, who looked wistfully at him and longed to follow him, but they ended by shaking their heads and going back to their old ways. This was the case not because they were not hungry of heart, but because they loved the praise of men more than they loved the praise of God. When I read that, I am on the point of stoning those ancient men. But looking at myself, my own arm becomes paralyzed as I say, "Lord, is it I?"

I am told that a good many years ago a boat of the Lee Line carrying a cargo of meat left New Orleans for the city of Memphis. That boat had not been long on its way before a boat of a rival company threatened to pass it. The captain of the Lee Line vessel felt that it would not be becoming to allow his boat to be passed by that of a rival company, so he ordered full steam ahead. This failing to get him past his rival, he thought of the cargo he was carrying. Therefore he ordered some of

IN PARABLES

the fat meat to be used to stoke his engines in the hope
of increasing their power. It worked so well that he resorted to that expedient again and again. At last with
whistles blowing and with flags flying he reached the
city of Memphis far ahead of his rival. That was all to
the good. But when the merchants came for their cargo,
they found that he had burned it up on the way. Now
the business of this captain was to deliver a cargo of
meat, but he allowed that to be crowded out by the
thorn of winning a race.

IV

How are we to avoid this tragedy?

There is only one way: We must put first things first.
Years ago a woman near my home was at the spring doing her week's washing. Suddenly she looked up from
her washboard to see that her home was wrapped in
flames. It must have crazed her for the moment, judging
by what she did. She dropped her washing and hurried
into the house and brought out an armful of quilts. Back
she went to drag out some pillows. Next she lugged out
a bed. Then the house reeled and staggered like a
drunken man and crashed into ruins. But louder than
the crash of the falling building was the wail of the
mother as she realized too late that her little child was
asleep in that house.

Now, it was surely no harm for this mother to have
saved quilts and pillows and beds. These are all innocent
and useful articles. But for her to have become so absorbed in such a task as to forget her child, that was
sheer tragedy. But a kindred tragedy threatens us. We

102

are all prone to allow the best to be crowded out by the thorns of second best. "And some fell among thorns, and the thorns grew up, and choked it, and it yielded no fruit." That is the story of a man with fine possibilities who went at last to meet his Lord with his hands as empty of usefulness as the pockets of a shroud.

X

EXCUSES

"And they all with one consent began to make excuse."

LUKE 14:18

THE PARABLE OF WHICH MY TEXT IS A PART HAS AN interesting background. Jesus is a guest at dinner. As he looks about him, he sees that his fellow guests and his host all belong to the same social and economic bracket. He recognizes the further fact that his host is not so much giving a supper as swapping one, just as we often swap presents at Christmas. Therefore he turns to his host with this word: "The next time you give a feast, invite the social nobodies, the underdogs, and not your kinspeople and rich neighbors. This you are to do lest"—and that word "lest" has a chuckle in it, also a dagger thrust—"lest they invite you and thus reward you for your supper. How that would break your heart!"

Now everyone present recognized the truthfulness of what Jesus was saying. That being the case, they were naturally a bit embarrassed. Their embarrassment, however, was not born of the fact that they knew they were guilty as charged. It was rather born of Jesus' blunt way of stating the case. When Hamlet told Polonius that the author he was reading declared that old men have weak hams and a plentiful lack of wit, Hamlet had no quarrel with the truthfulness of what he had read. He only declared that he did not think it was meet to have it thus put down. Even so, the host and guests here present did not dispute the accuracy of what Jesus had said. They only did not think it was meet for him to state it in his blunt fashion.

To save the situation, one brilliant guest rushed into the breach with a bit of pious twaddle that Jesus would have found positively laughable if it had not been so tragic. "Blessed is he that shall eat bread in the kingdom of God." What a prophetic utterance that was! The man who said it believed that this platitude would win such enthusiastic approval from Jesus that he would forget any further rebuke. But Jesus, with a smile on his lips and an ache in his heart, I think, answered, "If you think it is such a privilege to eat bread in the kingdom of God, why do you not eat it instead of doing everything else but?" Then as a sample of their conduct he told them the story of a man who made a great feast. If this is the same story that Matthew tells, it was a marriage feast and a royal marriage feast at that.

I

In this story Jesus by assumption makes at least three important affirmations.

1. He affirms that to enter the kingdom is a privilege. It is not only a privilege. It is the supreme privilege. In affirming this Jesus is speaking out of his own ex-

perience. He lived in the kingdom. He embodied the kingdom. By so doing he lived the richest, the fullest, the most abundant life that was ever lived on this planet. His, I take it, was the gladdest heart that ever beat in a human bosom, the sunniest face that ever looked out on this world. Jesus was a joyous man. The secret of his joy was that from the cradle to the cross he lived within the kingdom of God. His was a perfectly dedicated life. He could sum it up in these words: "My meat is to do the will of him that sent me."

2. This highest of all privileges, the privilege of entering the kingdom, is open to every human soul. In this story the invitation was first offered to the Jews. But before the story ends, the door is flung wide open to every man. The servants were sent out into the streets and lanes of the city, then out into the highways and hedges of the country. All men, without regard to their fitness, were invited. The kingdom is open to every human soul.

Therefore, to refuse to enter the kingdom is to refuse a privilege that we might claim if we were only willing. For God to invite and yet make it impossible for us to accept would be the most utter mockery and the direst cruelty. Whenever, therefore, we give any sort of excuse for our refusal to enter the kingdom, whenever we blame circumstances or blame anybody but ourselves, we are not telling the truth. This word— "Come; for all things are now ready," is flung out to every human soul. The highest of all privileges, the privilege of entering the kingdom, is open to every man.

3. A third assumption that Jesus makes is that this

106

invitation divides the invited into two groups, and only two. There were those who accepted and those who rejected it. That sounds autocratic and dogmatic, I confess. But be that as it may, there were only two classes then and there are only two classes now—those who accept and those who reject. There were some exceedingly unfit, yet who in spite of their unfitness accepted this invitation. There were others who, in spite of a far greater fitness, rejected the invitation. They refused by sending in their regrets. "And they all with one consent began to make excuse."

II

Now it is upon the silliness of the conduct of these people who sent in their regrets that Jesus wishes to focus our attention.

1. Their conduct was silly because they sought to be excused from an unmixed good. Had they sought to be excused from some needless danger or some useless moral risk, their conduct would have been reasonable. A young lady said some time ago, "I am constantly embarrassed when I go into the social circle by being offered a drink. I was brought up in an old-fashioned home where I was trained to total abstinence. Yet it is very embarrassing to me to have constantly to refuse."

"Well," I answered, "I might be somewhat embarrassed, but I do not think that I would suffer unduly. For instance, if I were to call at your home some afternoon and you were to say to me, 'We have been putting out rat poison recently, but we have saved back a little for sandwiches. Won't you have one of these nice sandwiches?' Under such circumstances I think that I would refuse. I believe I would say, 'I fear that I am allergic to rat poison. The truth is, I have known other rats quite as strong in will and quite as intelligent as I am who have died of the stuff. Therefore, if you will permit it, I beg to be excused.' "

When Daniel was carried away into exile in Babylon, he had not been in that strange city long before a great door of opportunity was opened to him. He found himself chosen, because of his good looks and intelligence, as a candidate for special work for the king. But no sooner was he in the king's palace than he was offered meat and drink that were contrary to his conscience. He might easily have said to himself, "Here I am in Babylon with a chance to get on, if I only conform, in spite of the fact that I am a captive. Therefore I am going to eat the king's meat and drink the king's wine. Everybody else is doing it. If I prove stubborn, I might not only miss my chance, but even lose my head." But instead of taking that course, he "purposed in his heart that he would not defile himself." Therefore, after all these centuries the one thing left standing in the city of ancient Babylon is the character of Daniel. If you excuse yourself from doing a wrong thing, you are wise, but what folly to excuse oneself from life's finest privilege!

Such conduct is as silly as it would be for a man starving to death for water to beg off when offered the privilege of kissing a lovely spring on the lips. It would be as if some man who was dying of hunger would beg as a special privilege that he be excused from eating. Here is a man who is dying of a horrible and torturing disease, and a physician tells him that he is able to heal

108

him, but instead of accepting the healing he begs to be excused. Here we are offered a place at the feast of life; surely no folly could be greater than to ask to be excused from such a high privilege.

2. These men who sent in their regrets were also silly in thinking that they could get away with such stupid alibis. Why did they send in excuses at all? They did so because they were conscious of the fact that they were doing wrong. We do not make excuses for our high choices, but for our low and mean choices. The very fact that they sent in their regrets indicated that they knew they were doing wrong. But while they were conscious of their wrongdoing, they thought that by these excuses they could conceal the wrong from their host.

What they were really undertaking to do was to please themselves without displeasing the man who had invited them. That is what many of us are trying to do. We want to please ourselves without displeasing God. When the prodigal ran away from home, he was not seeking to break his father's heart. He was not seeking an opportunity to waste his substance in riotous living. All he was seeking to do was to have his own way, to live his own life, to do as he pleased. We would like to do as we please, without displeasing God. Therefore we make excuses. An excuse is a sham reason that we give in an effort to cover up the real reason. A reason exists in itself. We never have to make a reason, but we do have to make an excuse. An alibi is always a manufactured article. Therefore it is always more or less false.

Look at the silliness of these excuses! One of them said, "I have bought a piece of ground, and I must needs go and see it." Another said, "I have bought five yoke of oxen, and I go to prove them." The excuse of the third was even more silly, "I have married a wife, and therefore I cannot come." What they are saying is this: "We are eager to come. We would give anything in the world if we could come, but it is utterly impossible. We cannot. Our absence, therefore, is not our fault. It is the fault of our circumstances."

Their excuses were obvious lies. They were silly, therefore, in thinking that they could get away with them.

3. They were silly in thinking there was any substitute for obedience. When you are invited to a feast, there is no substitute for accepting the invitation. This peddler of pious twaddle who said, "Blessed is he that shall eat bread in the kingdom of God," was making his twaddle a substitute for eating. What was wrong was not what he said. What he said was true. He was wrong in that he failed to practice what he preached. Some time ago I went to visit a woman who was a member of my church, but who had never seen me in all the months that I had been her pastor. When she discovered who I was, her tone became as unctuous as the ringing of church bells. She proceeded to tell me that what she longed to do above everything else was to work for the Lord. Then when I suggested a homely and simple task that she might do, she looked like a skyrocket making its return trip. She sought to make pious twaddle a substitute for obedience. There is no substitute for doing the will of God. To assume that there is, is merely to be silly.

EXCUSES

III

What is the danger of this habit of excuse making?

1. It is blinding. We make excuses in order to deceive others, but they seldom succeed in doing that. When I was a young chap and sought for the first time to honor a girl with my company, I remember her answer. It read as follows: "Please excuse me. I am too young to receive company." I was quite young myself and quite green and unlearned in the ways of society. But I had sense enough to know that it was not her extreme youth that robbed her of my company, but her unwillingness. Therefore I excused her. Had I not done so, there is no telling what a romance would have developed.

Excuses, I repeat, seldom deceive our fellows. They never deceive God. He looks on the heart. But the one they do deceive is the one who makes them. There is not a duty that we neglect, there is not a wrong that we do, that we cannot finally persuade ourselves is right, at least for us. I am talking to some who have left their church membership at Zion's Rest. But you have a good excuse. When you moved into this community, you did not know how long you were going to stay. Yet some have already been here twenty-five years. Besides, there is a sentimental attachment to the old church. Their step-aunt's baby is buried there, and so they leave their membership and forget their church vows.

Saul, the first king of Israel, confessed his sin more constantly than any other man in the Bible. But it never got him anywhere, because he always had an alibi. When, for instance, the prophet confronted him with the cattle and the sheep that he had stolen, he had a good excuse. He said that the people were to blame, that besides he had brought them along to sacrifice to the Lord. Therefore he had a high and religious motive for his failure to obey. Though he had been openly rebellious, he was in no sense to blame.

When Moses came down from the mountain, he found that weak-kneed Aaron had made the children of Israel a calf to worship. But when he called Aaron on the carpet, Aaron was not in the slightest to blame. He said that he had just cast a bunch of earrings and bracelets into the fire and out had come a golden calf. He implied that what happened surprised him more than it did anybody else. Naturally, therefore, he was not guilty. An excuse may not deceive the other fellow, it never deceives God, but it has a strange way of putting out the eyes and hardening the heart of the man who makes it.

2. The tragedy of thus blinding ourselves is that it shuts the door to improvement. If you have already arrived, you will not go any further. If you already know, you will not seek to learn. If you are already well, you will not consult a physician. If you are already good, you do not need a savior. If you have an excuse for your sin, then you are not a sinner. I have never known one man to move one inch closer to God until he quit making excuses and faced his own personal sin. It was when the prodigal came to himself and said, "I have sinned," that he took his first step toward a place at the feast of the fullness of life. Without that confession he could never have known again the fellowship of his father.

EXCUSES

3. The final tragedy of excuse making is that we miss the feast. If we desire to be excused, excused we shall be. Nobody has to accept. When Jesus was here, he looked after the milling crowds as he would look today, and said with an ache in his heart and a sob in his throat, "Ye will not come to me, that ye might have life." And so the king said, "None of those men which were bidden shall taste of my supper." Why? Because he had grown angry with them? No. Because he had shut the door in their faces? No. It was because by refusing to come they had shut the door in their own faces.

Now I dare to take the place of that servant of the long ago. I come to you with this greatest and richest and most bracing of all invitations, with this daring good news. "Come! for all things are now ready." God has made ready the feast without any regard to the cost to himself. The door stands wide open. You can enter now if you will. If you want to enter, nobody can prevent you. If you refuse to enter, God himself cannot compel you. What will your answer be?

113

XI

NOTHING TO SAY

"And he was speechless."

MATTHEW 22:12

MANY STUDENTS OF THE BIBLE HAVE DECLARED THAT the story of the guest without a wedding garment is a separate parable from that of the royal marriage feast. But while it is a separate parable, it has a common background. That is, everybody was invited to the feast. The invitation divided those who were invited into two groups. There were those who accepted the invitation, and there were those who rejected it.

All those who rejected did not reject in the same fashion. One group rejected with indignation and positive violence. This is hardly a common occurrence—for people to get angry over being invited to a royal wedding feast. Usually it is the folks left off the guest list who get upset. Yet it is a fact that God's invitation has stirred indignation and violence through the centuries. "Which of the prophets have not your fathers persecuted?" is a question put by Stephen. The prophets were constantly

114

giving God's invitation, and that invitation was often met by indignation and violence.

A second group of those who rejected the invitation did so with politeness. They did not wish to give offense. They were eager to remain on good terms with the king while they did as they pleased. Therefore they did their best to convince him that, while they were not coming to the feast, it was not their fault. It was rather because circumstances made their attending impossible. Therefore they sent the most appealing excuses that they could invent.

A third group, represented by this man without a wedding garment, did not reject either with violence or with politeness. He rejected by refusing to meet the conditions upon which he might enter the feast. He was all for reaching the goal, but he refused to travel the one road by which he could reach that goal. He refused the feast by refusing the conditions upon which the feast could be enjoyed. His sin, I take it, was the sin of presumption.

I

Now this is a very common sin. A certain wise psalmist prayed this prayer, "Keep back thy servant also from presumptuous sins." Even Jesus was tempted to the sin of presumption. In his fight with the tempter in the wilderness the first attack was made upon his faith. The tempter said in effect, "Inasmuch as you are the Son of God, command that these stones be made bread. Here you are in the wilderness. You are here at the call of God. You are here within the will of God. But if you do not look out for yourself, God is going to allow you to starve, even though you are within his will." But Jesus could not be thus led into doubt. Therefore he answered, "Man shall not live by bread alone, but by every word that proceedeth out of the mouth of God."

Then the tempter came over to the side of Jesus and even went beyond him. "You are right," he said, "in believing that God will keep you as long as you walk the path of obedience. Not only so, but he will keep you whether you are obedient or not. Not only can you trust him to keep you as long as you are faithful, but you can trust him to keep you even when you are faithless. Therefore cast yourself down from the pinnacle of the temple. That will be a spectacular and easy way to win attention. You can even do a foolish and wicked thing, and God will see you through." But Jesus refused to presume on God. Therefore he answered, "It is written again, thou shalt not tempt the Lord thy God."

Now since Jesus was tempted to this sin, it is by no means strange that such temptation comes to you and me. We are tempted to presume upon ourselves. We tell ourselves that we can get by where others fail. Thus some of us presume upon the laws of health and think that because we are well and strong we can do anything and continue to be well and strong. But sooner or later we find that our presumption has led us into trouble. I have buried quite as many strong men as weak ones. There is truth in the contention of Thomas Carlyle that the way to live to be old is to be afflicted with some incurable disease while young.

We often presume that we can get by dangers that would wreck others. For instance, some of us presume that we can mix liquor and gasoline with complete safety.

Of course we would be afraid to ride with the other fellow when he was drinking. Not only are we afraid to ride with him, but we are afraid to meet him on the highway. But with us it is different. We are at our best when we have had a drink or two. But even for us it is true that as our self-confidence rises, our efficiency goes down. Thus it comes to pass that every year we clutter up our highways with wrecks. This we do, not because we are vicious, but because we presume that we can get by where others have failed.

There are those who presume that they can sow without reaping. Of course other silly souls have to reap as they sow, but that is not the case with them. Jezebel is a case in point. She was brilliant, dashing, gifted, the Lady Macbeth of the Old Testament. She seemed to get by with her evil sowing for a long time. But at last the avenger is on her track, and even then she does not hide. She rather paints her face and decks herself in her best and takes a stand at the window. When Jehu comes, she preaches him a sermon. "Had Zemri peace, who slew his master?" she questions. Thus she seeks to remind him that Zemri had rebelled and had reaped according to his sowing. "Nobody gets away with anything," she declares.

"Right," answers Jehu. "Now by way of illustration—" then he shouts—"throw her down." There was a scuffle, a scream, and a dull thud. Thus even Jezebel, who presumed that she could hoodwink the laws of nature and gather grapes of thorns and figs of thistles, reaped as she sowed.

Then often we presume on one another. We believe that we can have friends without being friendly. We forget that life is a bit of an echo, that what you give you get. I use to lean on my plow handles and speak to a cliff across the Buffalo River. I discovered that I could get anything I wanted out of that cliff. If I wanted somebody to bless me out, all I had to do was bless the cliff out. If I desired a friendly boost, all I had to do was to give a friendly boost to the cliff. Emerson said, "If you want a friend, you have to be one." Don't presume that you can scorn the other man and make him love you, that you can neglect the other fellow and expect him to search you out and befriend you.

We at times even presume on our own loved ones. As I have married young couples across the years, I have tried to say to them, "You are very much in love today. Just remember that you will be far more in love twenty-five years from now, or far less." A marriage must be a growing relationship, or it will be a decaying one. There are many reasons why marriages fail. One of the most prominent is this—the husband and wife presume that because they have obtained a license to marry, their success is guaranteed. But this is not the case. I have a fishing license, but when I go fishing, I do not take my license from my pocket and shake it in the face of the bass and say, "Come and bite." My fishing license only gives me the privilege of trying to catch the fish. It is not a guarantee of a successful catch. Neither is your marriage license a guarantee that you will make a success. If through presumption you forget the courtesies by which you won each other, you are likely to wreck your marriage.

We often also presume upon our children. We recognize, if we are intelligent or thoughtful at all, that there is no substitute for training. There is no substitute for child care. Therefore we look after their physical and intellectual needs. We see to it that they go to school. Somebody must teach them reading and writing and arithmetic. But we are not careful, many of us, in teaching them spiritual values. We do not teach them about God as revealed through Jesus Christ. They must be specifically taught in other matters, but we can depend upon mere chance to teach them the supreme lessons of life. Such presumption is turning loose a hoard of lusty pagans who are causing endless trouble and heartache. We cannot afford to presume upon our children. If we do, we will never get another chance. There is one thing that does not have a next time, and that is the rearing of a boy or a girl.

Most tragic of all, many even presume upon God. "Behold I stand at the door and knock: if any man will hear my voice, and open the door, I will come in." That is a beautiful and winsome promise. Yet many expect God to come in whether they open the door or not. But God never "poaches upon the sacred precincts of personality." If we do not open the door, God will not and cannot come in. A man said some time ago, "I believe that God will save the average, and I am as good as average; therefore, I believe he will save me." That is sheer presumption.

We believe in the forgiving love of God. That is the very heart and center of our gospel; yet some of us presume on that. In a Georgia city some time ago a young married woman asked me for an interview. She told me of her disagreement with her husband, of her falling in love with a married man, who himself had a lovely wife. They had not gone the limit, but she was trying to get me to say that it would be, in a sense, right for her to do so—that what was adultery for other people would not be adultery for her. And then she came out with this remark, "Even if it is wrong, when it is all over I can repent." Well, perhaps she could, but I doubt it. Anybody who commits sin with her eyes wide open, with such willful presumption, is liable to become incapable of repentance. We presume on God.

II

Look how it worked in the case of this man without a wedding garment. I can imagine myself among the guests on that fateful evening. There I met this friend and said, "I see that you accepted the invitation."

"Indeed I did," he replied. "I had no thought of missing this finest of all life's opportunities."

"But," I asked, "where is your wedding garment?"

"Oh," he answered, "I haven't any, but I'll get by all right." But at that instant the king came to see his guests. No sooner had he entered than his gaze was fixed upon this man. Then, not in anger but with great tenderness and pity, he asked, "Friend, how camest thou in hither not having on a wedding garment?" What did the man answer? He answered nothing at all. The consciousness of his sin of presumption struck him dumb.

Why did he not plead ignorance? Why did he not say to the king, "I have no wedding garment, it is true, but I did not know that a wedding garment was necessary." Had such been the case, he certainly would have given that answer. But he could not. He knew the conditions upon which he was to enjoy the feast. He knew that everybody had to have a wedding garment. But though aware of this, he presumed that he would be an exception.

Another answer that he would have gladly given was this: "I knew that I had to have a wedding garment, but I thought this garment of mine was a wedding garment. It looked to me quite as good as that of the other guests. Therefore I thought that I had met all the conditions." If such had been the case, you can count on it, he would have given that answer. But he could not. He knew two facts about the situation. He knew the conditions upon which he could enter the feast; he knew also that he had not met those conditions.

Yet another answer he would gladly have made was this: "Your Majesty, I knew that a wedding garment was necessary. I also knew that I did not have a wedding garment. But I simply could not obtain one. I certainly desired one. Indeed I would have given my right arm, I would have given my very life for one, but my eagerness was of no avail. Therefore, though I am unprepared for the feast, the fault is not mine." But he could not say that. He knew the conditions. He knew he had not met the conditions. He knew that he could have met them if he had only been willing.

As to what this wedding garment represents, it is needless to argue. Some say that the king supplied the wedding garment. Whether or not that was true of this ancient feast, this I know: it is true of the gospel feast. Salvation is a gift. The wages of sin have to be earned. "For the wages of sin is death; but the gift of God is eternal life through Jesus Christ our Lord." When we are

121

willing, God gives us the gift of salvation, which is the gift of himself.

To those who thus receive him the door to the feast opens of its own accord. In the face of all others it is shut. This is the case because they simply would not fit in. They do not belong. Therefore they would be more wretched on the inside than they would without. Let us bear in mind that an invitation to the feast means an invitation to meet the conditions upon which we can enter. Let us do this even now, earnestly praying this prayer: "Keep back thy servant also from presumptuous sins."

XII

A DRAMA OF THE HIGHWAY

"He had compassion on him, and went to him."

LUKE 10:33-34

HE . . . WENT TO HIM." THAT IS THE SIGNIFICANT fact. Compassion is good, but it is not enough. I feel quite sure that the priest and the Levite were sorry for this wounded man, but their pity was not dynamic enough to drive them into action. They simply said, "Poor fellow," and went on their way with the resolve to pray for him, perhaps, when they got home. But the Samaritan went to him. It was a dirty, bloody, costly job, but he knew that he could save the man in no other way. Even salt, if it does its saving work, must give itself to the thing to be salted.

The story of which this text is a part is one of the most gripping that Jesus ever told. In fact, it has won its way into the heart of humanity as none other with the exception of the parable of the prodigal son. That still remains the most beautifully tender and the most tenderly beautiful ever told. But this runs it a close second. It is a drama of the highway. It brings us face to face with flesh and

123

blood people like ourselves. We meet three groups on this ancient road, as we meet three groups on the road which we travel. The first group is made up of those who are wounded; the second, of those who wound; the third, of those who heal.

I

Let us look first at the wounded. This man lying half-dead by the roadside represents a great company. Who is he? Frankly we do not know. The robbers have stolen his card case. We do not know his color, or his race, or his nationality. We do not know the language which he spoke. We do not know whether he was cultured or ignorant, whether he was rich or poor, whether he was a man in the early springtime of life or an old body coming close to the sunset and evening star. All we know about him is that he was a man who had been robbed and wounded.

He was left thus nameless because he represents just anybody and everybody. He is one of the casualties of the road. There are many of us. In fact we all play that role at one time or another. However we may put up our defenses, sooner or later we are among the wounded. I do not wonder, therefore, that John Watson said to a company of young ministers as he was coming close to the end of his life, "Be pitiful, my young friends, for everyone is having a hard time." I do not wonder that the Lord of the bruised reed enabled his prophet to say, "God hath given me the tongue of the learned, that I should know how to speak a word in season to him that is weary." Traveling this Jericho road is a bit like walk-

124

ing over a battlefield after the battle, with the cry of the wounded in our ears.

Of course we are not all wounded in the same fashion. Some of us may be wounded economically. There may be want where there was once plenty. Sometimes we hear people minimize the worth of money. Now it is altogether easy to overestimate its worth. But Jesus never spoke of money with contempt. Whenever I hear one so speaking, I know that it is very likely that such a one doesn't know what it means to be penniless. At the close of my first year in college when I received my allowance on which to return home, I found that it was a bit more than I needed. Therefore I resolved to visit the ocean since I had never seen it. Having put that resolve into execution, when I returned I no longer had more than I needed, but less. I was able to buy my ticket, but if in the coming days I did not fast and pray, I certainly did the former with a vengeance. In a small way I learned what it was to feel the pinch of hunger.

There are some of you who are wounded in your bodies. Health has given way to sickness. Or perhaps you are wounded in your self-respect. Something has happened that has humiliated you and has lowered your morale. Or you may be wounded in your affections. There is a loneliness where there was once a companionship. Or you may be wounded in your spiritual life. In the rush of things you have somehow let slip the hand of your Lord, and today you are saying, "As the hart panteth after the water brooks, so panteth my soul after thee, O God." I do not know just how your wounds were inflicted, but they are painfully real whatever their causes.

125

Then there are those whose wounds are the result of their own wrong choices. When we look in their direction and realize something of their suffering, we often seek to excuse ourselves by saying, "Yes, he is in a bad way, but he has nobody to blame but himself." Often that is true, but the fact that I have nobody to blame but myself does not make my lot easier; it only makes it harder. If I can look at my painful wounds and say, "Yes indeed, they are painful, but I received them in the way of gallentry and honor," they will not be so hard to endure. But if I have to say, "Yes, I am deeply and desperately wounded, and that, not because I was heroic, but because I played the fool," then my agony will be far greater. Some of us are wounded by our own wrong choices.

There are those of us whose wounds are evident to all whom we meet. Anybody can see that life, in some fashion, has dealt harshly with us. There are also those whose wounds are hidden. I have always loved the story of that Samaritan king, who, when his city was shut in by a besieging army and life had grown hard, was accustomed to take a stroll every day upon the walls. This he did in order to keep up the morale of his suffering people. I can imagine that at first they looked at him with approval and applause. But as life grew hard and as little children continued increasingly to pluck at their skirts asking for bread that they could not give, their approval gave way to disapproval. At last they looked at him with eyes hard with envy and resentment. "Oh, yes," they said, "it's easy for you to parade like that, but you do not know what we are suffering."

Then something happened that changed their attitude entirely. Something happened that made their hard eyes grow tender with unshed tears. What was it? They got a glimpse through the rent in the royal robe of their king and saw that he wore sackcloth within upon his flesh. They thus came to realize that he too was suffering, that he was bleeding from a hidden wound. We are all sooner or later among the casualties. The fact that we are here does not mean that we have escaped. It rather means that we have been picked up instead of passed up.

II

A second group that we meet on this Jericho road are those who wound. They are divided into two groups.

1. First, there are those who wound aggressively. These are represented by the brigands. These men, possibly a score, were hiding in the fastnesses of the mountain. They looked down and saw a lone traveler. When they saw him, they said, "There is a man at our mercy. There is a man of whom we can take advantage." Therefore, with no thought of the suffering of their victim, with no thought of those who would wait in vain for his return, they sprang upon him, took his wealth, and all but took his life. Then they hurried away to their hiding place. They wounded aggressively.

Of course, we feel no kinship with them. We would never any more think of laying hold of a man and taking his wealth by violence than would this priest and Levite. Perchance we might take it by chicanery. We might take advantage of his ignorance, saying to ourselves, "Business is business." I never heard a man use that expression except one who had just beaten somebody out of something or was seeking to do so. A chap told me with genuine zest some time ago that he had been able to buy a gun worth $150 for only $10. When I asked how he found such a bargain, he replied that a rather intelligent Negro man had recently died in his community, leaving this fine gun. "I went," he boasted, "and offered his widow $10 for it. Not knowing its value she accepted." Naturally, I could not help wondering why he did not steal the gun outright and save himself the $10.

Sometimes we wound aggressively with our tongues. We hear a choice piece of gossip and pass it on. Of course, it is true or we would not have heard it. "There cannot be so much smoke without some fire." That is another saying that is a symptom of a deadly disease. When we employ it, we are usually asserting that we have just heard a bit of scandal and have fervent hopes that it's true. Some wound aggressively.

2. Second, there are those who wound passively. We can break heads with a club; we can break hearts with neglect. These people are represented by the priest and the Levite. When they saw this wounded man, their reaction was essentially the same as that of the brigands. The first thought of the brigands was of themselves. Here is a helpless man; what can we get out of him? The first thought of the priest and Levite was of themselves. They knew that the robbers might be hiding not a hundred yards away waiting for another victim. They knew also that even if this was not the case, to help this half-dead man would be quite troublesome. Therefore, thinking first of themselves, they passed him up.

Now of these two types our Lord seems to have regarded those who wound and rob passively as the more dangerous. Such a course is more dangerous to those who are guilty. This is the case because it is often possible for us to do nothing and not feel guilty in the least. It was the realization of this fact that caused our Lord in his parables of judgment always to denounce those who did nothing rather than those guilty of some aggressive wrong. Then he denounced such for a second reason. He knew that to refuse to help one who is wounded may prove to be as deadly as an aggressive attack. So often all that is necessary to wreck any man or cause is simply to do nothing.

For instance, if you own a farm and you want to turn that farm back into wilderness, it is not necessary that you sow it with weeds or plow furrows down the hillside. All you need to do is to let that farm alone. If you want to wreck your church, you do not have to slander your pastor, you do not have to run him out of town, you do not have to throw stones through the window. All you have to do to wreck any church is to let it alone. Just pass it by. Do nothing. If you have a growing boy, and you want to lose your boy, you do not have to teach him to lie and steal. All you have to do is not to teach him anything. Send him to school to learn reading, writing, and arithmetic, and depend on him to reach up in the skies and get the Sermon on the Mount and the Ten Commandments and a sense of the values that last. Very often all that is necessary to wreck any person or thing is to do nothing.

Why were these two decent and religious men guilty of such deadly and damning conduct? It was certainly not because they were religious. The easy assumption of certain fiction writers that pagans are paragons of virtue while the average churchman is a scoundrel is not founded on fact. The church represents a slight majority of our present population, but it does over ninety percent of the giving. If I am a worldling and you are a churchman and if we are just average, you give nine times as much as I do. These men did not fail because they were religious; they failed in spite of their religion.

One reason, perhaps, that they passed this man up was that they were tired. They had just concluded a meeting in Jerusalem and were now on their way home. Then in all probability they were busy men. They doubtless had other engagements down in their home city. Besides, helping this wounded man was not one of their appointments. Nobody had assigned them to such a task. Thus this was an off-duty duty. That is about the sharpest test we meet on the road. It used to shock me to read the harsh words of Jesus about our having to account for every idle word. But I have come to realize that the idle word is the revealing word. The idle word indicates what we are. We are more apt to reveal ourselves when we speak off the cuff than when we speak for publication. Even so there is no sharper test than the off-duty duty. There is nothing more revealing than what we do when we come face to face with human need with nobody looking on but God. These two men did not meet the test. Therefore they had to take their place in the prisoners' dock along with the brigands who had robbed the man.

III

The third group, those who heal, is represented by this Samaritan. By common consent the University of Humanity has conferred upon this man the highest possible degree. It is so far higher that it makes the degree of doctor of philosophy or master of sacred theology look like doll rags. That degree conferred by common consent is the title "good." Jesus did not call him the good Samaritan. Those who have read his story through the centuries have given him that title. And that, I submit, is the highest degree that can be conferred upon any man. Not only so, but it is the highest degree that can be conferred upon God himself.

> Yet in the maddening maze of things,
> And tossed by storm and flood,
> To this fixed trust my spirit clings:
> I know that God is good.

Here then we see goodness in action. It is significant that we call him good, not by a single thing that he refused to do. We call him good because of what he did in the presence of human need. When he saw this wounded man by the roadside, the effect the sight had upon him was exactly the opposite from the effect it had upon either the robbers or the priest and the Levite. They thought first of themselves. When the good Samaritan saw him, he thought first of the wounded man and of himself not at all.

Bear in mind, too, that he did not have a single advantage that the priest and the Levite did not have. He had no more skill as a physician. He had no more wine and oil. He had no more appointment with this wounded man than they had. All he had was a more vital interest. When he saw him, he had compassion on him. When he saw him, it was love at first sight. Not that he had at once conceived a fondness for this battered and bruised and horrible-looking wreck. He rather fell in love with him in the sense that Jesus means for us to love. He was gripped by a good will for him as a man, a good will that was aggressive and sacrificial. It was so aggressive and sacrificial that he could not pass him up. Therefore he went to him and bound up his wounds, pouring in oil and wine.

Nor was this simply a passing emotion. There are those who will do good on the spur of the moment, but who will soon weary and give over the task. This man could follow through. So he put the poor chap on his horse, and steadied him as he walked at his side all the way to the little inn around the bend of the road. Arrived there, he had to lose a nights' sleep waiting on him. Then the next day he took out certain money and gave to the innkeeper and said: "You see him through. And if you need anything more, if the wounded man himself is worth his salt, he will pay you when he recovers." No, he did not say that. He said, "I am going to take it all on myself."

What became of the man who was wounded? I do not know. He may have been back on the same road and no better off a year from that time. But that was not the business of the good Samaritan. His business was to help him when he had the chance. If we have to find out what will be the outcome of all those whom we seek to help before we give aid, we shall never give any.

132

This man may have become a pillar in church and state. He may have appreciated what his rescuer did for him with a gratitude that knew no bounds. On the other hand he may have proved a renegade and an ingrate. But, be that as it may, he had his best chance at the hands of the man who helped. Not only so, but the man who helped did what everybody feels that he ought to have done.

Therefore we are not surprised; therefore we feel that it is altogether fitting, when our Lord turns to us who are also traveling the Jericho road and gives this sane word, "Go, and do thou likewise." Every man knows in his heart that this is the way he ought to use life, that this is the way he himself could use it if he were only willing. "And when he saw him, he had compassion on him and went to him." We can do much through organized charity. We can do much over the long distance telephone. But if we are to give help in the superlative degree there is no substitute for personal contact. There is no substitute for the giving of ourselves. So I close with the word of our Lord, "Go, and do thou likewise."

XIII

THE LAYAWAY PLAN

"Here is thy pound, which I have kept laid up in a napkin."

LUKE 19:20

"HERE IS THY POUND." THE MAN WHO UTTERED THAT word has no light in his eye, no thrill of immortal music in his voice. He has made a mess of things. Not only so, but he knows he has made a mess and that through his own fault. There are those standing about him at this moment with light in their eyes and a lilt of victory in their voices who have had exactly the same opportunities that he has had. They made something of those opportunities while he threw his own away. His tragedy was not in any positive wrong. He tried to use the lay-away plan, and that is one that never works.

I

This parable of the pound introduces ten servants, but in reality only three of them come actively upon the scene. Only three are in the limelight. There are two respects in which all of these servants were alike.

134

First, they were alike in that they all received the same gift. Here this parable parts company with the parable of the talents. In the latter parable the first man received one talent, the second two, and the third five. Each received according to his ability. That points out a distinction in the abilities of men. We are not all created equal in our capacities whatever the Declaration of Independence may say. Now and then some chap will affirm flippantly, "I can do anything that anybody else can do." Of course that is as silly as it is false.

There are many things that others can do that I cannot do. There may be some one thing that I can do that they cannot. Even small children can do what we cannot do. On the train a few years ago I noticed a little chap not over four years of age who had remarkable skill in drawing. His artistry so fascinated me that I got acquainted with him. In fact we became so well acquainted that he invited we to draw him a picture. Determined to be a good sportsman, I asked, "What shall I draw?" And looking me over, he answered with a wisdom beyond his years, "Draw me a mule."

Now, if there was a man on that train who should have been able to have drawn a mule, I was that man. I almost qualify as a mule specialist. I was raised with them. I have plowed them. Perhaps at times I have even preached to some and had a few on my official board. I was really a mule expert. But when I set myself to the task and drew the very best mule that I could, it so offended the artistic soul of my young friend that he was on the verge of tears. The only way that I could maintain my self-respect was by telling myself that I did not claim to be an artist anyway. We cannot do everything that anybody else can do.

But there is one respect in which we, as Christians, are all alike. We have all received the gospel of Christ which is the power of God unto salvation. We have all been recipients of those glad tidings of great joy that are for all people. We have all come to possess eternal life through Jesus Christ our Lord. We have all received the gift of salvation which is none other than the gift of God himself. We are alike in that we all have equal access to God. The invitation is flung out to every one of us, "Come boldly unto the throne of grace, that we may obtain mercy, and find grace to help in time of need."

After the death of Moses, "the Lord spake unto Joshua, the son of Nun, Moses' minister, saying, Moses, my servant, is dead; now therefore rise, go over this Jordan, As I was with Moses, so will I be with thee." When God gave that promise, he did not tell Joshua that he would make him into another Moses. If he had wanted another Moses, he would doubtless have kept the one he had. He simply meant that he would be as real to Joshua as he was to Moses. He meant that he would make Joshua into his best possible self.

God is giving that same promise to you and me. He promises us the power to do his will and to carry out his purpose in our lives. That is perfection. Nobody can go beyond that. Paul declared that he was out to lay hold on that for which he had been laid hold of by Christ Jesus. In proportion as he succeeded in that high enterprise, in that proportion he fulfilled the will of God. So God, in offering himself to us, enables us to carry out his purpose. In order to do the will of God all you need is God. All God needs is you. We are all alike, therefore, in that we have received the gospel of the grace of God.

A second respect in which all these servants were alike was this: that they all received the same command. "Occupy till I come," says the King James Version. "Trade with these till I come," says the Revised Standard Version. That is, every man was to take the capital put into his hands and put it into circulation. They were to venture it on the marts of trade. They were to use it in the service of others. We were created and redeemed for usefulness. No man is condemned to the hell of uselessness. "Go ye and make disciples," is the command, not simply to a chosen few but to every Christian. When Paul said to his timid friend Timothy, "Do the work of an evangelist," he was giving a command that is for you and me as well. Every man is to take what God has put into his hands and into his heart, and use it in the service of others. They all had laid upon them the same command, "Trade with these till I come."

II

Now if there were two respects in which they were alike, there were also two respects in which they differed.

First, they differed in the use they made of the gift that was put into their hands. They differed in the degree of loyalty to the command of their master. One man went and traded with such wholehearted diligence that his one pound became ten pounds. Now, I do not take this to mean that he became ten times as strong a Christian as he had been before. I do not take it to mean that he won a certain number of converts. I think ten stands for approximate perfection. That is, this man was wholehearted in his loyalty. Humanly speaking, he did his best. He was therefore graded one hundred percent.

The second man took the command of his Lord so seriously that he also went earnestly to work. But though he worked with diligence, he did not do quite as well as he might have done. He represents a far greater company than the first. He represents most of us. I said to a company of ministers the other day that ninety-eight percent of us do not preach half as well as we could. We have some earnestness. We put some energy and enthusiasm into our task. But few of us do our approximate best. But this man worked so earnestly that his one pound became five. Therefore he received a passing mark and was not thrown into the discard.

This third man did not use his pound at all. That does not mean that he set no value upon it. He valued it highly. He sought with some degree of earnestness to keep it. He made the mistake in trying to do the impossible. He thought that there was a possibility of keeping something that he would not use. That is contrary to the laws of nature. When the apple tree in my orchard blossoms, either an apple follows or the blossom comes to nothing. The greatest pianist of a generation ago discovered that if he refused to use his music for a single day, he himself could tell the difference; if he refused to use it for as much as two days, his hearers could tell the difference. There is no virtue and no value that we can keep by using the lay-away plan. This man sought to keep his pound without using it.

Differing in the use they made of the treasure put into their hands, they also differed in their reward. The man who had done his approximate best received the highest reward, ten cities. The second received in proportion to his capacity. The last man also received in proportion to his capacity. The door opens to every one of us that we have fitted ourselves to enter. In our faces every other door is shut. Even God cannot give us what we are not capacitated to receive. This man, as every one of us, received the reward for which he had fitted himself. Thus there were two ways in which all these servants were alike. There were also two ways in which they differed.

III

Now, it is upon the face of the man who used the lay-away plan that our Lord focuses the spotlight. Why did he use such a plan?

It was not because of ignorance. He had heard the command of his master just as plainly as his fellow servants. Nor, I repeat, was it entirely because of indifference. He really desired to keep the treasure that had been put into his hands. No more was it fear. That was what he himself claimed. He declared that his fear of his master kept him from using his pound. But his master refuted that and proved that that was an excuse rather than a reason. I think it is true that fear played an important part in the failure of the man with one talent. When he thought that as much might

139

be required of him with his meager gifts as of his fellows with their far greater gifts, it paralyzed him. As we say, "It scared him stiff." Therefore he did nothing.

But it was not fear that defeated this man. It was rather an absence of fear. He was so bold and presumptuous that he did not take his master seriously. He thought that he could find a substitute for obedience. For this reason his master called him a wicked servant. In what respect was he wicked? He was wicked, not in that he had squandered his pound, but in that he had refused to obey. "To him therefore that knoweth to do good, and doeth it not, to him it is sin." There is no substitute for obedience. It is by the door of obedience that we enter the kingdom. It is through obedience that we live the life of the kingdom.

When Naaman came to be cured of his leprosy, the prophet commanded him to dip in the Jordan seven times. Such a command made the general indignant. The story says that he went away in a rage. Why was he so hot about it? "Because," he declared, "if it is a matter of dipping in a river, then I might dip in one of the rivers down at Damascus. They are far superior to this dinky little Jordan. Dipping in Jordan simply does not make sense." Therefore he sought to make his own plan a substitute for obedience, but he found that it did not work.

Saul, the king of Israel, confessed his sins more often than any other man in the Bible. Yet he ended by losing his crown and losing himself. He was always seeking a substitute for obedience. One day when caught in the very act of rebellion, he had a fine substitute. He offered some fat cattle and fat sheep. But the prophet

140

said, "Behold, to obey is better than sacrifice." There is no substitute for obedience. The command of God is that we are to take the pound that we have and trade with it. If we do not, we disobey and therefore lose our pound.

Christianity is in its very nature aggressive. Jesus said it was like leaven. The property of leaven is not that it goes as a small minority into a great majority of meal and holds its own. Its property is that it changes the meal. Jesus said of his disciples that they were salt. Now salt is an aggressive something. It is the very opposite, the very antithesis of the negative and the neutral. Salt, if it is desired and is not present, leaves a lonesome place against the sky. Then when salt shows up where it is not wanted, it can be terribly in the way. Jesus meant by this that being a disciple makes one different. If you make no difference in your community, in your church, in your home, then whatever else you are, you are not a Christian.

The Christians of the early church understood this as we do not. Therefore they never allowed themselves to be put on the defensive. When Stephen was being tried for his life, indeed when he was being executed, he did not seek to defend himself. He went to the attack. In fact he went to the attack so vigorously that a young man named Saul received a wound in his heart from which he never recovered. Then years later when this man Saul, now a Christian, stood up to defend himself before Agrippa, he forgot to defend himself as he went aggressively to the attack. He so proclaimed his gospel that Agrippa had to sneer in order to keep from sobbing. Whenever a Christian ceases to be aggressive, he ceases to be in reality a Christian.

As a young chap, I did some football coaching. I was no great shakes as a coach, but I at least knew this much, and I tried to drill it into my team, that we would never make a touchdown while the other side carried the ball. That is something that every Christian needs to learn. You will never make a touchdown while you allow the world and the flesh and the devil to carry the ball. If Christianity is not aggressive, I repeat, it becomes a pale and anemic thing. You have all the drabness and the grayness without any of the glamour and the glow and the thrill. It is only as we aggressively adventure that we can know the joy of the Lord which should be our strength.

Now, it strikes me that this parable puts its finger on the sore spots in the lives of so many who are in our churches today. These are thoughtful, well-wishing people. They are not bad. They do not do any special harm. But the type of sinner of which our Lord was always most afraid was the man who was good without being good for anything. Dives was not a bad man. He was far more kindly, I daresay, than his neighbors. He was so kindly that he allowed a beggar to lie at his very gate. But one day, in his pride over his goodness and decency, he hung his silken sandaled foot in the rags of that old beggar and fell out into the night. This was the case not because he had done the beggar any wrong, but because he had refused to do him any good. Unless we are aggressive, we just have the drabness, I repeat, without the glow.

Now if that is your condition, there is a way out. I

142

can assert that with absolute confidence. Some years ago I had a very fine and gracious gentleman as a member of my church. He was more or less in earnest in his efforts to be a Christian. But his religion, as he himself confessed, was a form rather than a force, something to be put grimly through rather than to be enjoyed. But by the utmost pressure I induced him to go with a friend to do some personal evangelism. He went with great reluctance. A few days later I heard that timid, retiring man whose religion had been a bit of a bore give a thrilling testimony. There was a new light in his face and a new ring in his voice. He spoke after this fashion: "If a man had told me a few months ago that God would ever do through me what he has done these past days, if he had told me that I could ever have the assurance in my heart that I have at this moment, I simply could not have believed him. But as I have ventured, I have found by my own experience that the promises of my Lord are true."

I could believe what he said because of the radiance of his face. I could believe it also because it was in complete harmony with the promises of Jesus. He is saying to you, to me, to every man, "If any man will to do his will, he shall know." All you have to do to make your life a miserable failure and to lose the treasure from your fingers is nothing. But if you desire to increase your treasure and to find for yourself and others a growing spiritual certainty, adventure it. Then the results will be sure. And may God lead you every one to begin in the here and now.

XIV

GOD AND MONEY

"You cannot serve God and money!"

LUKE 16:13 (Goodspeed)

Y OU CANNOT SERVE GOD AND MONEY." THIS JARRING
text is the climax of one of our Lord's most impressive stories. This word sounds like a threat, but such is not the case. It is not primarily a warning; it is a plain statement of fact. Of course, we do not have to accept it as a fact. Millions have refused to do so. They have been convinced that they could make the best of both worlds, that they could give allegiance to two masters. But by so doing they did not wreck this fact; they only wrecked themselves. "You cannot serve God and money."

I

This text confronts us with a choice. It brings together two values with which we all have to do—God and money.

Money—that is a charming word. At least it is in the market place, at the bank, at the store, in the

144

real estate office. It is "as musical as dreambells sounding on the sloping hills of sleep." But somehow when we hear it in the sanctuary it loses its winsomeness. For many it becomes as jarring as musical instruments played out of tune. There are some who fairly gnash their teeth as they say to themselves, "Money, money, money! That's the way it always is when I come to church."

Such people are not in the majority, thank God, but they are always with us. I used to have a wealthy old bachelor in my congregation. His money was his wife, his children, and all his in-laws. Therefore, when I would preach a sermon on money, he would come forward to tell me that though I had made a fairly good address what he liked to hear was the old-time gospel. But that is just what he had been hearing. No man can preach the gospel and ignore money.

A few years ago a group of excellent women asked for the use of our sanctuary to hold a worship service. When we granted their request, we also indicated where they could find the plates for the offering. But they drew back from this suggestion as if we had told them where to find a case of choice liquor. "This is to be a worship service," they said with a note of horror. Thus they implied that an offering would make a worship service impossible. But an offering is a fundamental part of a worship service. Any service that is too sacred for those participating to give an offering is too sacred to pray the Lord's prayer, or to read the Shepherd Psalm, or to sing "When I Survey the Wondrous Cross."

Sad to say, this squeamishness about money is not

145

confined to the pew. There are even ministers who shrink from proclaiming the gospel of money. I once had a pastor, an excellent man, who declared sincerely that he did not think that a discussion of money had any place in the pulpit. I was once pastor of a church whose boast was that their former pastor was so deeply spiritual that he never mentioned money in the pulpit. I could only answer that he must have been very spiritual indeed since he had run past Jesus. Not only did our Lord mention money, but he had more to say about money and matters related to money than any other subject on which he spoke. That this should be the case is not amazing. We do not live in castles in the air; we live in a homely world where we have to handle values represented by money every day. Therefore, if we do not learn to relate ourselves aright to money, we simply do not learn to live.

Personally, through the years I have preached on money without apology. Not only so, but I have preached on it with genuine joy. I still do so. I love to see the liberal enjoy such preaching, and I love to watch the stingy suffer. But in all sincerity only a very small part of my enjoyment is sadistic. I truly believe that Jesus was right when he said, "It is more blessed to give than to receive." If I were asked to present you with a lovely gift, I would do so without any pain, apology, or embarrassment. Commanded by my Lord to offer you a yet greater privilege, that of giving, I also do this without apology or embarrassment. In urging you to give I am doing you a favor. I am calling upon you to do that without which you cannot really live.

Here our Lord confronts us with the choice between

God and money. If we put money first, we of necessity leave God out. The young ruler was an earnest, courageous man. Jesus cast a veritable spell over him. He admired Jesus no end. He was eager to follow him. There was only one other object for which he was more eager; that was his wealth. He gripped it. He was also gripped by it. As he went away grieved, he began at once to discover that while money might be a good servant it was a hard and hellish master.

Over against the claims of money stand the claims of God. If the mention of money in the sanctuary shocks and grieves some, such is not the case when we speak of God. His name is one that is quite at home in the pulpit. But if we really make God our choice, if he is really our Lord, his name must be at home everywhere. To make our loyalty to God a thing of holy days and holy places is to defeat his purpose for us altogether. God must be as much at home in the market place, in the shop, factory, and store, as money. We are to handle the tools of our daily work as religiously as we handle our hymnbooks at the hour of worship. Our choice then is between God and money, God and all the so-called secular.

II

The crook who stands at the center of our story put money first. He did it so decisively and with such clear-eyed abandon that his master, though cheated by him, had to commend him for his shrewdness.

He was shrewd in that he could make a wholehearted choice. His yes to one way of life was a 100 per cent yes. His no was also a 100 per cent no. He was the very opposite of that donkey that stood between two bundles of luscious hay and starved to death because he could not decide which one to eat first. He did not try to keep step with two bands that were playing different tunes. He was a man of decision.

Having made his choice, having decided to provide for the material needs of his future, he drove straight to his goal. Perhaps a friend, perhaps his wife, told him that in using his master's money to provide for his future he was forfeiting his honer. But he answered, "What of it? I am after money. Of course, I would get it honestly if I could, but since I cannot, I am still going to get money." Therefore, he proceeded to make rich gifts to his master's debtors, using for these gifts a wealth that was not his own.

Being thus a man of one purpose, set only upon providing for his physical needs at any cost, he succeeded in the enterprise upon which he set his heart. He made his tomorrow as secure as money could make it. Some to whom he had given wealth became his friends out of gratitude. Those who refused to become friends because of gratitude were made friendly because of fear. Those latter had become partners in a dishonest deal. They had shared his stolen gains; therefore, if appreciation of his kindness proved ineffective, then there was still blackmail. Thus he made friends and thereby provided for his future by the shrewd use of his master's wealth.

It is told of a certain governor that he gave a considerable sum of money to his private secretary, a young woman in her twenties, to deposit for him at the bank. But this young woman instead of making this deposit in the name of the governor made it in her own name. When he heard of this glaring bit of dishonesty on the part of his secretary, he did not have her arrested. He did not even fire her in disgrace. Instead he commended her in that she had acted shrewdly. In fact, he promoted her to be treasurer of the state. He appointed her to an office where millions of dollars would come into her hands every year. Not only so, but he had a law passed that she was to audit her own books.

Even so I am confident that this crook succeed in providing for his tomorrow beyond his expectations. I feel sure that instead of being fired, he found himself more secure in his position than he had ever been before. I have no doubt that his employer, who was himself a rascal, said, "Any man who can steal thus shrewdly from me might as well steal a little for me. He is entirely too resourceful to lose."

Here then is the case: Confronted by a choice between God and money, the rascal of our story chose money. He chose it wholeheartedly. By having thus chosen he made good. He was no doubt rated a successful man. I dare say hundreds commended him by declaring one would have to get up early to run past him. But there is this sad fact—he is not a success any more. All his ill-gotten gains slipped from his fingers long centuries ago. He won a temporary victory, but he lost the war.

III

Our Lord offers another and higher choice. Instead of putting money first we are to put God first.

Now if we do this, it does not mean that we withdraw

from the world and live in a cloister. It is perfectly right to make money. "Not slothful in business," is the word of Paul. Having made money it is perfectly right to seek to conserve it. Waste is not only silly; it is also wicked. No man has a penny to throw away. Not even God has a crust of bread to waste. When Jesus fed the multitude, he said, "Gather up the fragments that nothing be lost." It is just as religious for the God-called businessman to make money as it is for the God-called minister to preach, given the same motive. If God is put first in the pulpit and in the market place, then both preacher and businessman are rendering their highest possible service.

Suppose, then, we should put God first. What would it have to do with our handling of money? Jesus answers by three clear contrasts.

1. It would enable us to take what is another's and to change it into our very own. Now, all we have is another's. No man owns anything. "The earth is the Lord's and the fullness thereof." Among the first convictions that came to the saints after Pentecost was this: "No man said that ought of the things he possessed was his own."

Since God owns everything, we are to acknowledge his ownership by the setting aside of a certain portion of our substances to be used for his service. What proportion are we to set aside? The only one suggested in the Bible is the tenth. In Old Testament times any Jew who refused to tithe was charged with robbing God. In the New Testament there is a higher law of giving called stewardship. But stewardship, which means the using of all our wealth as God shall lead, is the

150

graduate school of giving. We are not likely to get into this graduate school unless we enter by the high school of giving, which is tithing. Therefore Jesus gave his approval to the giving of the tithe. He did so when to have refused that approval would have made the point he was making more telling.

"Ye pay tithe of mint and anise and cummin," he declared, "and have omitted the weightier matters of the law, judgement, mercy, and faith." The natural thing for him to have said after this was, "All your tithing is of no value since you neglect the weightier matters of the law." But he did not say that. Instead he declared that they should have practiced justice, mercy, and faith without neglecting to tithe. The same is surely true for us. In tithing, therefore, we are doing something that we have had no right to leave off. Who said so? Jesus.

If we thus tithe as an act of faith and obedience, we let God into our daily task. He becomes in a profound sense our partner. We make it possible for him to open the windows of heaven above our heads and pour us out a blessing. Thus dealing fairly with God in the use of our possessions, we win what is our very own. By thus obeying we grow increasingly in Christlike character. That is a wealth that is truly ours. It is a wealth which no one can take from us.

2. In thus using our money we change it into true riches. Of course, money in itself is of no value. A $10,000 bill in itself would be worth no more than a $1 bill. Neither would be worth anything in supplying the real hungers of the heart. One reason our Lord called the rich farmer a fool was because he thought

he could feed his soul on corn. But the right use of money does change it into true wealth. When the knight in "The Vision of Sir Launfal" shared his crust with a beggar, we read that the soul of the beggar stood out in his eyes and that he stood before him glorified. Indeed he was no longer a beggar but the very Christ himself. By thus sharing, the knight changed his material bread into the bread of life.

3. Finally by using our money aright we can change what is temporal into what is eternal. Jesus puts it this way: "Make to yourselves friends of the mammon of unrighteousness; that, when ye fail, they may receive you into everlasting habitations." That is, we can take our material wealth and change it into friends. This is a fact of experience in our present world. Look for instance at the gracious ministries of the Fuzzy-Wuzzy angels in the South Seas during World War II.

> Many a lad will see his mother,
> And husbands see their wives,
> Just because Fuzzy-Wuzzys
> Carried them to save their lives
> From mortar or machine-gun fire,
> Or chance surprise attack,
> To the care of waiting doctors
> At the bottom of the track.
>
> May the mothers of America
> When offering up a prayer,
> Mention these impromptu angels
> With the fuzzy-wuzzy hair.

How can we explain these "impromptu angels"? How

had these savages been changed into friends? Somebody had given money for the support of certain missionaries who had come to this needy field. Thus they had changed money into friends. If we can do that in the life that now is we can also do it for the life that is to come. What is the one something in this world that is going to last? Human personality, nothing more. Dives thus had his chance of making a friend of Lazarus, but he passed it up. Therefore he found himself in eternity alone. Nothing could be more tragic than that.

Such need not be the case with you and me. If we as an act of faith, obedience, and love give of our money, we can make friends in the here and now both for ourselves and for others. Not only so, but we can thus change our wealth into friends that will greet us on life's other side. "You cannot serve God and money." That is true, but under God we can make money serve us and others both now and forever. Thus money that is called unrighteous because it so often leads to evil may be a means of the highest good. Though symbolizing the material it is still a solemn trust. In fact there is nothing more sacred than the so-called secular.